M000169437

It Happened In
Las Vegas

Twenty-Five Remarkable Events
That Shaped History

Paul W. Papa

Guilford, Connecticut

Copyright © 2009 by Morris Book Publishing, LLC

Project editor: David Legere
Layout: Sue Murray
Map: M. A. Dubé © Morris Book Publishing, LLC

Library of Congress Cataloging-in-Publication Data is available on file.
ISBN 978-0-7627-5017-7

Printed in the United States of America

10 9 8 7 6 5 4 3 2 1

Special thanks go out to Ray Jones, without whom this book would not have been possible, and Carole O'Keefe, who acted as a sounding board and kept my grammar on track. This book is for Donalyn, who never stopped believing.

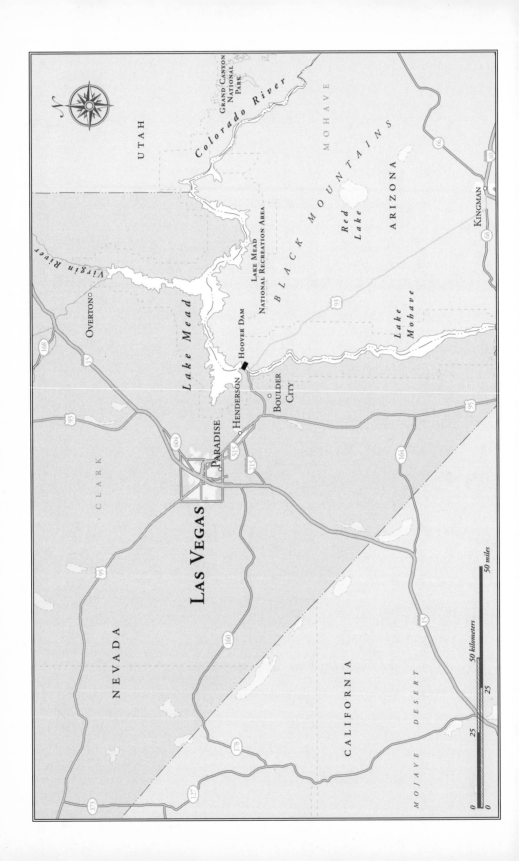

CONTENTS

CONTENTS

ACKNOWLEDGMENTS

I want to especially thank the many employees and volunteers at the Las Vegas museums who helped so greatly in the research of this book and the many residents who took the time to tell me their stories. I treasure those moments. I would especially like to thank the Atomic Testing Museum, the Neon Museum, the Clark County Museum, and the Nevada State Museum. I would also like to thank the Old Las Vegas Mormon Fort State Historic Park and the University of Nevada Las Vegas Special Collections.

INTRODUCTION

Las Vegas is a fascinating place to live. Nowhere else are people as encouraged to come and leave their inhibitions behind as they are in Las Vegas. The city can treat a person to the spoils of Rome one day and the cafes of Paris the next. It is the only place in the world where you can walk from New York to Egypt and back, all in one afternoon. It doesn't care who you are, what you do for a living, or what you call yourself . . . it just invites you to come, and it lets you call it Vegas.

A drive from the airport to the Strip will expose visitors to billboards full of half-naked people alongside major stars. Vegas is one of the last places where you can stay in the same hotel as a celebrity or rub elbows at a gaming table. It is a town where you are almost expected to get into trouble. And having done so, know that not only will it be okay, but the town will keep it secret.

Las Vegas is a town only one hundred years old that in many ways is still trying to find itself. Starting as a Western gambling camp, it has evolved into a major resort destination, reinventing itself many times along the way. Las Vegas is known for discarding its past, like most people discard clothing, imploding buildings with little care for their historic value. Yet it preserves its precious neon signs and it keeps a death grip around other parts of the past that had an arguably small impact on the town—such as Las Vegas's fascination with Elvis Presley.

It is called "Sin City," but Las Vegas also has a strong religious community and was founded, at least in part, by a major religious organization, one that has a strong presence in the community to this day. Unfortunately too many people visit Las Vegas without enjoying its spectacular scenery and wonderful natural resources. But when a town promotes gaming and entertainment as much as Vegas does, what can you expect?

Opulence is king in Vegas, and I have chosen many stories to show that in particular. However, Las Vegas has always been a town that made its own path, not necessarily being worried about the perception of other people or other towns. And in my humble opinion, that is what makes Las Vegas special. So I have also chosen stories that show the pioneer spirit that I feel has never left this town. As I said, it is a wonderful place to live and I hope that these stories give you a taste of just how special this little town really is. Enjoy.

MORMONS ARRIVE IN LAS VEGAS

1855

William Bringhurst stopped to wipe the beads of sweat that dripped from his forehead and gathered on the back of his bright red neck. The scorching June sun had taken a heavy toll on the bodies and spirits of him and his twenty-nine men. For the past thirty-five days they had pulled, dragged, and pushed forty ox-drawn wagons, fifteen cows, and a few horses through some of the harshest rocks ever assembled into a mountain range. Still, receiving a mandate from their leader Brigham Young, the men braved the more than 100-degree temperatures to settle the valley that would eventually be called Las Vegas.

The corners of Bringhurst's mouth formed a wide grin as he looked out over the vision that opened before him. Sharp rocky cliffs had been replaced with lush green fields and fresh running water. Bringhurst and his companions may have looked over the valley that lay before them and rightly wondered if it was simply a mirage created by the hot desert heat, or if they had found a paradise in the desert. The men quickened their pace and even the animals seemed a bit more spry as the group approached a creek of fresh clear running water. The vision hadn't been a mirage. They had finally arrived at their destination, a valley of green swaying grass and sprouting trees that the Spanish had named The Meadows. Their journey had come to an end and now they could start the work they had come here to do.

It's strange to think that a city built on vices would have its roots in religion. But such is the case with Las Vegas. The thirty men who arrived in the valley on June 14, 1855, were members of the Church of Jesus Christ of Latter-Day Saints (LDS), known as Mormons. The group, led by Bringhurst, had been sent to the area by Brigham Young, the leader of the LDS Church, to protect both the mail and the pioneers who were making their way west.

Almost since their founding in 1820, the Mormons had a difficult relationship with the U.S. government. It all began when their founder and first prophet Joseph Smith claimed to have spoken with God himself and to have translated golden tablets he received from an angel. Certainly there were those in government positions who found these claims to be a bit of a threat to their power structure.

Whether or not the claims of Joseph Smith were true, they served as a catalyst that put the fledgling church in direct controversy with members of local government. In fact, the church seemed to gather enemies almost as quickly as it gathered converts. Mayors turned to governors, who themselves turned to the United States to help rid their communities of the pesky Mormons.

While the LDS Church started in New York State, persecution forced its members to keep heading west in search of a place where they could practice their religious beliefs in peace. Government policies (the governor of Missouri signed an order to exterminate them) and mobs pushed them out of Ohio, Missouri, and eventually Illinois. In the winter of 1846, after the murder of their beloved prophet Joseph Smith two years earlier, Young started them on a migration to what would eventually become the state of Utah.

It took the LDS pioneers more than a year to make the trip through the rugged Rocky Mountains, paving trails as they went and doing so largely with handcarts. The trail they created became a major trading and travel route known as the Mormon Trail. In July 1847, Young looked over the valley of the Great Salt Lake and declared it to be "the" place. He claimed most of the Great Basin, including an area that would eventually become part of the state of Nevada. Young petitioned the U.S. government to name his newly formed territory Deseret, but the United States rejected his proposed name and instead named the territory Utah after the Native American Utes who inhabited the region. The naming showed that although the LDS Church had largely escaped oppression, it had not escaped its uneasy relationship with the United States.

Young set up a community, establishing a city he named Salt Lake. But Young's vision for the area did not stop in the Salt Lake valley. He continued to send groups of pioneers west, settling all areas possible in the Utah Territory, eventually reaching all the way to California. Young knew that water was an essential element for survival and so he sent out groups to settle mainly where water was plentiful. He also knew the church and its members couldn't survive without a steady flow of income, and he had an idea.

Communication in the 1800s was done mainly in the form of letters and packages that were given to wagon trains as they went westward. But a new form of transportation had taken hold of the west, making it much easier to get mail. Letters were placed in saddlebags that were then carried by small, fast-moving horses across the plains to the west. Called the Pony Express, the service was looking to expand to California and Young wanted that passage to go through the trail his members had created.

The U.S. government awarded a contract to the Mormons for carrying the mail westward to California. When the United States allocated funds to build a military road on the Mormon Trail, Young took advantage of the opportunity and sent Bringhurst to establish a settlement post in Las Vegas.

Young chose the valley for several reasons. It was almost exactly halfway between Salt Lake and San Bernardino. The area was named Las Vegas "The Meadows" by the Spanish because the valley had an abundance of free-flowing water and lush green grass. Young presumed the area could be easily irrigated, making it easy to grow crops. The area was already an established resting place for tribes of Native American Paiutes and traders.

Having quenched their thirsts and those of their animals, Bringhurst and his men searched for a place to build a structure they could use as a fort. The valley was still unsettled, and while the Native Americans were reported to be peaceful, the Bringhurst party feared the possibility of attack from Mexican nationals who still roamed the area. Bringhurst chose a hilltop located a short distance from the springs. The hilltop was flat enough to sustain a structure and the spot allowed the group to foresee any approaching attackers. The thirty men drove their oxen to the hill and unloaded supplies from the wagons, including the material they needed to build the fort. While building the fort was the priority, Bringhurst also intended to contact the Native American Paiutes, teach them how to raise crops, and bring them the word of God.

Bringhurst sent men out to find large stones that could be used as the foundation of the fort. As the stones were found, they were brought up the hill on wagons and laid out. With the fort underway, Bringhurst established relations with the Paiutes. "We agreed to treat them well and they were to observe the same conduct towards us." Bringhurst appointed George W. Bean, who spoke the Paiutes' language, as a translator. Bean worked well with the Paiutes and through his conversations with them learned how to make bricks of sun-dried mud, called adobe. The bricks were used to build the walls of the fort. Bean reported back to Young that "the [Paiutes] were soon partially converted to habits of industry and helped us grub the land, make adobes, attend the mason, and especially to herd the stock."

When the 150-square-foot fort was complete, it had walls that stood 14-feet high with bastions positioned on the northwest and southeast corners. The men also cleared mesquite trees, planted crops, and built cabins with wood from the nearby mountains. While the fort had an encouraging beginning, it was doomed almost from the start. The soil in the area was extremely alkaline and even though water was plentiful, the men found it impossible to grow crops. They were also unaccustomed to the searing heat that baked the valley. In fact, the heat was one of the main reasons the Paiutes did not have a constant presence in the area. The group had also chosen possibly the worst time to settle, arriving at the beginning of the hottest time of the year. What few crops the settlers did manage to grow were almost completely destroyed by the unencumbered sun. One settler wrote: "The prospect for the land looks slim. Most of the wheat is badly blasted."

The Paiutes themselves did not help the quickly dwindling situation. They didn't see any problem with freely taking the white man's crops for their own needs and did so on a regular basis. By the time the first winter arrived, all but seventeen of the settlers had returned to Salt Lake. Bean remained and one day while talking with the Paiutes discovered that they knew of lead deposits in nearby Mount Potosi. Bean reported the find to Brigham Young, who sent

Nathaniel V. Jones to the mine to determine if the ore could be removed and shipped to Salt Lake. Jones arrived at Mount Potosi and began the work of mining the ore.

As the ore came from the ground, Jones ordered his miners to mold the lead, but found it "very hard to smelt." The frustrated Jones tried over and over again to pour lead into molds but every time the molds were opened, the lead cracked. Unfortunately, what the inexperienced Jones didn't realize was that he was not working with pure lead, but a mixture of lead and silver. Not realizing that they had been mining a precious metal, Young ordered them to abandon the mine in January 1857, leaving the discovery of silver for other settlers.

Young "realized the spirit of the mission was broken," according to Bean, and made the decision to abandon the fort. In February 1857, Young wrote a letter authorizing the brethren to return to Salt Lake. "Although some remained behind, the last of the settlers finally left the valley when the Paiutes took the remaining crop." While the fort may have been unsuccessful, the road the Mormons established remained a major travel route to California. The remains of the fort were eventually purchased by the State of Nevada, which operates it as a museum. The LDS Church eventually returned to Las Vegas and grew in membership, building a temple in 1989.

THE SALE OF LAS VEGAS . . . AGAIN

1905

Anticipation filled the hot May air as more than three thousand bidders and spectators stepped down the metal stairs of trains, eager to make their fortunes. Some people were dressed in fine silk hats with expensive suits and cravats. Others wore weather-battered shoes and dusty jackets covered in mud. They traveled from as far away as California and Salt Lake. The host of the event, William Clark, offered round-trip transportation from Los Angeles and Salt Lake at $16 and $20 respectively. He also promised to refund the travel money for anyone who purchased what he was selling—Las Vegas.

Bidders made their way to a pine stage that had been quickly assembled for the event. The stage was covered on the top and back by white canvas and stairs had been built onto one side. Men gathered on the stage, paperwork spread out onto the table in front of them. Dust filled the dry air and the temperature had already reached its 88-degree average. The cotton-clad bidders had no choice but to crowd as close to the stage as possible, struggling to take advantage of the limited shade.

The auctioneer on stage slammed a gavel hard on the table, creating a puff of dust. He rambled in a fast singsong of half-words emphasizing, at key moments, the prices bid by the spectators. People held up cards and yelled out prices, making bids of up to $1750 for a plot of land. The auction progressed quickly, building excitement as prized plots became scarce. When the last swing of the gavel crashed on the pine stage, Clark had sold 176 of the 1,200 lots, making $79,566, and there was still another day to go. But this wasn't Clark's biggest problem. Unbeknownst to most of the bidders that day, the townsite of Las Vegas had already been sold a year earlier.

Since 1881 rumors had been spreading that the railroad was planning to connect Salt Lake to the fast-growing Los Angeles. The rail was slated to follow the Old Spanish Trail, now called the Mormon Trail, which ran through the valley known as Las Vegas. The owners of the Union Pacific Railroad, seeing great opportunity for advancement and profit, installed the rails along the trail. Unfortunately the railroad was not operated well in the 1880s and fared no better when the financial panic of 1893 hit the United States. By the time the Spanish-American War erupted in 1898 the Union Pacific was on the verge of bankruptcy. It eventually reorganized, but not before a competitor bid and won the rights to the area.

That competitor was William Andrews Clark. Born in Pennsylvania in 1839, Clark was motivated by nothing more than greed and a desire to make a lasting impression on the world. Clark moved with his Scotch-Irish parents to Iowa when he was seventeen. There he studied law and taught school. He served on the Confederate side of the Civil War until 1862, when he started drilling a mine in Tail Hill, Colorado.

William Clark had a younger brother named J. Ross Clark who was a banker and successful miner. J. Ross moved to Los Angeles for health reasons and opened a sugar beet factory, which was a new industry to the Los Angeles area. It was J. Ross who first approached his brother with the idea of forming a railroad and running it from Salt Lake to California. The railroad would not only be able to move quartz and copper from Montana, it could move sugar beets, newly discovered gold and silver in Nevada, and anything else that needed to be transported to and from the Southwest.

The brothers formed the San Pedro, Los Angeles & Salt Lake Railroad. Clark knew that the railway would need a place to stop and water the steam boilers of the engine, so he searched for a place where water was plentiful. The Las Vegas valley was the perfect choice. Not only did it have an abundant supply of water, it was a halfway point between Los Angeles and Salt Lake. While investigating the area, Clark discovered that a rancher was willing to sell land for the purposes of establishing a railroad, so he set up a meeting.

Helen J. Stewart owned a large ranch in the area that was once the Mormon Fort. Her husband had seized the property in an 1882 foreclosure. Before he was shot and killed in a gunfight in 1884, he had managed to turn the site into a large ranch that stretched almost two thousand acres. Clark met with Stewart and told her of his intentions to bring his railroad to the valley. Stewart was pleased and in 1892 sold Clark the rights to 1,840 acres of the ranch for $55,000. The deal did not include four acres of a family burial ground or a separate lot of 160 acres that Stewart would keep in the family. What the deal did include was the all-important water rights.

Clark purchased the land with the initial intent of creating a water station, repair shops, and houses for workers on his railroad. However, following his more ambitious desires, he quickly realized that the spot was the perfect location for a town. All Clark needed to do was survey lots and sell them. Enter John T. McWilliams, a Canadian emigrant born in 1863 who had moved to the United States in 1879 to pursue a career in engineering. McWilliams had apprenticed as a surveyor in Canada and took up the career when he needed to find a job. McWilliams had a very successful career, being appointed as a delegate to the National Irrigation Congress in Los Angeles, designing Flagstaff, Arizona's first water system, and surveying the Bright Angel Trail into the Grand Canyon. In 1902, Clark hired McWilliams to survey the 1,840 acres Clark had purchased from Stewart four years earlier.

As McWilliams surveyed the land, he was struck by the same thought that had entered the head of Clark: that the spot was the perfect location for a townsite. Being a surveyor, McWilliams certainly had the ability to lay out streets, blocks, and sidewalks. With the idea in his head, McWilliams approached Stewart and was able to talk her into selling him half of her remaining 160 acres in the west portion of the ranch. What Stewart was not able to sell him was the water rights that had already been purchased by Clark. It was a factor that would prove to be an issue down the road.

In 1904 McWilliams advertised his new townsite, which he called "McWilliams Townsite," with the promise to make money quickly: "Get in line, buy now, double your money in sixty days." He offered low prices, easy terms, and promised to make public improvements once the railroad arrived. McWilliams's vision paid quick dividends, as sales through the winter months grew. By 1905, the area boasted a population of almost two thousand, with thriving stores, saloons, and bakeries, most of which were in tents, helping the site to earn the nickname of Ragtown. McWilliams's townsite even had three weekly newspapers. But as the town grew, water became scarce. Because Clark owned the water rights to the ranch, the residents of Ragtown were forced to get whatever water they could from wells.

Although McWilliams had beaten him to the punch, Clark was not about to let his plans be stolen by the surveyor he had hired. Clark divided the east side of the ranch into thirty-eight identical blocks of land to form the Las Vegas Townsite. The blocks measured three hundred by four hundred feet and had eighty-foot-wide streets with twenty-foot-wide alleyways. Blocks 16 and 17 were designated for the sale and consumption of alcohol. Block 20 was zoned for a library and courthouse.

Clark even went so far as naming the streets—Fremont, Carson, Bridger, and, of course, Clark—names that still hold today. Clark initially offered the lots at $100 to $300 an acre. But when he was overwhelmed by more than three thousand offers, his natural greed kicked in and he saw an opportunity to generate even more money by changing his plans. He canceled the early agreements and set up a two-day public auction to be held on May 15 and 16, 1905. McWilliams was furious with Clark's promotion and took out an advertisement warning prospective buyers that "auction sales are never good for the buyers" explaining that "people get excited at auctions and feel like kicking themselves the next day." McWilliams's warning would go unheeded.

On the second day of the auction, the scene from the previous day repeated itself. With dust in the air, auctioneers rambled, bidders raised their signs, and Clark felt confident that all of his remaining plots would sell. He was almost right. While not every plot sold, Clark managed to make a grand total of $265,000 on the sale of Las Vegas.

Within hours of the end of the two-day event, people moved their tents and temporary wooden structures from McWilliams Townsite to Clark's side of the railroad tracks. The local newspaper, the *Las Vegas Age,* rolled its fireproof building to Clark's Las Vegas Townsite and the Imperial Hotel tore down its building only to reassemble it stick by stick on the new townsite's more prestigious property.

McWilliams continued his fight in a vain attempt to save the area he insisted be called the "Original Las Vegas Townsite." He advertised in the same Los Angeles papers as did Clark. But a lack of water rights and frequent fires proved to be too much for the struggling townsite. While the fires didn't completely destroy the site, it never recovered. McWilliams built his own house in the townsite and eventually won the water rights for his eighty acres, but his dreams of development were never realized and he died in 1951.

While McWilliams never successfully developed Las Vegas, the property he owned in Spring Mountain, later called Mount Charleston, was eventually developed into the recreation area called Lee Canyon. Clark fulfilled his dream of leaving his name behind when on July 1, 1909, Lincoln County was split into two: Lincoln and the newly formed Clark County. The Las Vegas townsite established by Clark is the area currently known as downtown Las Vegas.

THIS IS SAM'S TOWN

1906

Several men leaned against a bar drinking and sharing stories. Others filled spaces around them, trying to get the bartender's attention, while the piano player pounded the keys in the corner. As more and more men entered, the saloon quickly became overcrowded. Drunken men pushed into even more inebriated men and tensions heated. As is often the case when alcohol is involved, one man said something to another and offense was taken. What started out as words quickly erupted into fists.

Sam Gay heard the commotion as he walked by the saloon. He pulled up each sleeve one at a time and tugged the lapels of his jacket. Then, without hesitation, he pushed through the front doors, grabbed the closest drunken man and flung him out the front door behind him. Gay swiftly moved his size thirteen boots through the crowd, wasting no time, and shoving men aside as he went. When he found the two men who had started the confrontation, he took hold of them by the back of their necks and swiftly pulled them apart. Then, just as swiftly, he slammed them back together, their heads smashing into each other with a dull thud.

While momentarily stunned, the two men continued to struggle. Gay pulled them backward and slammed them back together, harder than he had the first time. The men dropped to the saloon floor, where, after a moment of confusion, they again continued the fight on the ground. Gay took hold of their collars and headed for the front door, dragging them out of the saloon. Once outside he tied the two together over a hitching post. He filled a bucket with water and threw it into their faces. With the fight finally out of the two men, Gay untied them and sent them on their way.

The scene was an almost nightly occurrence in the Las Vegas of 1906. Having been organized only a year earlier, Las Vegas had already turned into a bustling community. It had its own municipality, including a police and sheriff department. It also had an area of town where law was not so heavily enforced and vices ruled. Known as Block 16, the area was created by William Clark in 1905 as a place where alcohol could be served without a license. Block 16 quickly became a wild part of town where fights broke out nightly and killings were commonplace.

Enter Sam Gay. Born in Canada in 1860, Gay grew up in Massachusetts where he worked on a farm until, like many at that time, the promise of fortune called him west. Gay moved to California and then Alaska, chasing gold in 1900. When that proved unsuccessful, the frustrated Gay returned to California and took a job as city marshal in Coronado, California. At the ripe age of forty-five, Gay was approached by the owner of the Arizona Club in Las Vegas, who offered him a job as a bouncer in the now infamous Block 16.

Gay was an imposing figure. He stood six feet tall and weighed 260 pounds. He was reported to have hands that were twelve inches long and wide. Gay didn't believe in carrying a gun. Instead he preferred to handle confrontations by hand, and it was a heavy hand indeed. Gay acted quickly when a confrontation arose. It was not uncommon for him to slam combatants into each other just to get their attention. Gay did his job so well that in one short year he became the night watchman for the entire Block 16.

Gay didn't see his job as one that required the enforcement of laws. Instead he saw it as being more to prevent men from killing each other. But just because he didn't enforce laws that didn't mean he allowed too much ruckus. On one occasion Gay marched sixteen men out of town. The men were seen walking fast, trying to avoid being kicked in the behind by Gay. "He kicked one with the bottom of his foot, and just lifted him right off the ground," recalled Leon H. Rockwell, an early settler.

Gay brushed aside claims that the men should have been arrested. "I saved the state and county a lot of money." Gay knew that the men would have been tried, convicted, held, and eventually released. "We'd have fed them until they got the wrinkles out of their bellies. Now these men will never come back as long as I am here." Gay was right; the men never came back.

Gay did just as much to help people from getting hurt as he did stopping men from getting rowdy. Known in the community as "Big Sam," Gay routinely told people the parts of Block 16 that should be avoided, even giving one person a gun, because he worried the man was going to be in a dangerous area unprotected. Gay was very much a live and let live person, so long as things were going smoothly and nobody stepped too far out of line.

From the time of its creation Las Vegas had been part of Lincoln County. However, in 1909 Lincoln County was split in two, and Las Vegas became part of the newly formed Clark County. Charles C. Corkhill, editor of the town's newspaper, the *Las Vegas Age*, was elected as the county's first sheriff. Corkhill wasted no time in appointing Gay as his first deputy sheriff. However the partnership was not made in heaven.

The main problem was that Corkhill wasn't much of a lawman and Gay was more concerned with keeping the peace than enforcing the laws. Gay was also more practical than Corkhill. On one hot sunny day in 1910, Gay noticed that the men in the overcrowded and rat-infested jail were suffering badly from the heat. The men were sweating heavily and had trouble staying awake. The jail was made from sheet metal and railroad ties and could reach temperatures inside of over 117 degrees. Gay knew that heat exhaustion could be deadly, so he chained the sweaty and exhausted men together and took them down to the old Las Vegas Ranch where he sat them under a cottonwood tree for shade. When Corkhill found out he was furious. He fired Gay on the spot. Later that same year Gay ran against Corkhill for sheriff and beat him.

In many cases, court had been held in the blacksmith shop of the justice of the peace Jacob Ralph. To temper metal Ralph kept a large tub filled with water. When Ralph would put the hot metal in the tub, the water would overflow and splash onto the ground. This created a muddy pool that Ralph's ducks loved to wade in. Gay brought arrested strangers into the court. As court was held the ducks would quack, making it difficult to distinguish the quacking of the ducks from the voices of the witnesses. This was just fine, because Justice Ralph didn't pay much attention to the witnesses anyway. When Gay brought a stranger before the justice, Ralph would ask how much the stranger had in his pocket and pronounce a fine of that amount.

As Las Vegas grew so did the need for a new jail. A new building was built that had two rooms, one painted blue and one pink. The "blue room," as it was called, was for housing male prisoners, while the pink room was only big enough for a single female prisoner. Even after the jail was built crowding remained a problem. Those convicted of minor crimes were often given a choice to either go to jail or take a "floater," meaning they were put on the first train out of town.

In 1911 Sam Gay became the first elected sheriff of Clark County. Being sheriff allowed Gay to continue his own brand of law enforcement. He broke up fights and kept the death rate low. He was so well respected that he was also appointed the chief of police for the Las Vegas Police Department. One of the reasons Gay understood the needs of the men to "let off a little steam" was because Gay himself was prone to do the same thing. It was not uncommon for Gay to sit in his office next to the library, slam down a few drinks, and break into rather questionable song. This did not sit well with the conservative ladies in the library.

Gay also had a tendency to shoot things when he became intoxicated. On one occasion in 1915, Gay staggered out of his office onto Fremont Street and looked dreamily up at the shining lights. He unholstered his gun and shot out the lights. The stunt got him in trouble with the district attorney Albert Henderson. Instead of admitting to the charges or defending himself, Gay instead swore that "so long as I am sheriff of Clark County, I will not take a drink of intoxicating liquor. If I do, I will hand in my resignation." It was a promise he kept.

One morning Gay was met on the street by Marjorie Schaeffer, a five-year-old girl who handed him a box and scurried away. The box marked "Sheriff Sam" contained a solid gold badge. The words "Sheriff, Clark County, Nevada" were inscribed on its face. "Compliments of Las Vegas friends" was inscribed on its back.

Sam continued off and on as sheriff until 1930 when he retired at the end of his term. While the town would most likely have elected him again, Gay complained that too many crooks were coming to Las Vegas. "I've dealt with honest men so long, I wouldn't know how to act around crooks."

In the summer of 1932, Gay was in California. He ran to catch a streetcar and suffered a minor heart attack. When he returned to Las Vegas that August, he was struck again, only this time the heart attack took his life. He was sixty-eight. Hundreds of people attended the funeral services of Big Sam Gay. Al Calhan, a journalist for the *Evening Review-Journal,* wrote: "Sam Gay numbered his friends by the thousands, and was always the friend of the underdog. He had a following that was loyal almost beyond belief, and that, more than any words I might say, constitutes a eulogy complete." In the winter of 1932, when Sam Gay was laid to rest, his gold badge was placed in his hands.

BOOTLEG CANYON

1920

Men hid behind a group of rocks as the sky filled with a shower of rock and dust. The blast created a large opening in an even larger rock. No sooner had the dust settled when the men scurried to the rock and augured out a hole in the top with a large hand drill. When the hole was finished, a metal tube was placed inside to act as a smokestack. With the tube in place, the men directed their attention to the opening they had created with dynamite. They removed rubble from the opening and unloaded equipment from the Model T that transported them up the dusty trail into the canyon.

Buckets, tubes, and containers were placed next to the opening, along with a large stack of wood. An old box spring was positioned on the other side. Wood was stacked under the equipment and used to fuel a fire. Select ingredients were placed in a type of crockpot and positioned over the flame. Smoke rose up the tube as the production of illegal alcohol, otherwise known as moonshine, began in the small canyon just outside Las Vegas.

Up until 1920 alcohol had been produced by large companies that distributed their product to saloons. The saloon, predecessor to the modern bar, was a common fixture in the American West. Saloons had increased in number since 1890 when companies such as Pabst and Anheuser-Busch began the production and distribution of lager beer, which had been brought to the United States by German immigrants. While it was no problem to have several different bottles of alcohol, such as whiskey, on the shelves, it was not as practical to have many different kegs of competing beer on tap.

To help get their product to a wider audience, beer brewers began to build and support saloons that only carried their product. This marketing strategy dramatically increased the number of saloons in the United States. At one count there was one for every 150 to 200 people. Saloons were becoming too common and, worried about their effect on morality, the Anti-Saloon League started a movement to get rid of them. Carrying the motto "The saloon must go," the league brought their message to community churches of all denominations.

While the program grew steadily, the league realized that to be successful they needed to take their fight to the national level. They knew that the only way the league would be able to rid local communities of the saloons was a national law prohibiting the sale of alcohol. To garner the national attention they needed, the league organized a march that they were sure would put pressure on the U.S. government. On December 10, 1913, four thousand members gathered in Washington, D.C., to march down Pennsylvania Avenue.

The league combined with other organizations, including the Woman's Christian Temperance Union, and eventually turned the tide. On January 16, 1919, the Eighteenth Amendment to the U.S. Constitution forbade the manufacture, sale, or transportation of intoxicating liquors in the United States and its territories.

The news hit the bustling area known as Block 16 especially hard. Established in 1905 as the only place licensed to sell alcohol in the town of Las Vegas, Block 16 had become somewhat of a legend in the American West as a place where a man's vices could be catered to. If alcohol was taken out of the equation, the saloon owners in Block 16 feared their other businesses, namely gambling and prostitution, would dry up as well.

The resourceful citizens of Block 16 refused to let the amendment discourage them. Instead of losing their livelihood, they chose to ignore the new amendment and fund the production of illegal bootleg alcohol themselves. Just forty miles outside Las Vegas was a small, narrow canyon that would serve as the perfect place to set up production operations. The canyon was nestled between two large hills with plains on either side. Access was gained through a small dirt trail. The plains were flat and climbed gradually to the hills, making it virtually impossible to access the trail without being seen.

Crews of men went into the canyon where they set up their alcohol-making equipment in holes blown into rocks. Many stayed in the canyon, setting up camp, in order to make sure that no one stole their alcohol, or moved in on their site. Production quickly proved successful. The alcohol was placed in jugs and bottles, and transported from the canyon to Block 16. Customers walked to the back or side of the saloons and exchanged their money for alcohol. "The front door was locked and you had to go around the back of them to get in," recalled Las Vegas resident Theodore Garrett. "There weren't signs, but everyone knew without signs. It was such a situation where 'You pay me and I'll keep quiet.'" Leroy Burt, another resident of Las Vegas, recalled "You'd go around the side and knock on the door, they'd sell you a pitcher of beer for fifty cents." The program worked so well that the trail to the canyon became known as Bootleg Road.

The production of alcohol became so popular that it was impossible to keep it quiet. In no time alcohol was sold openly inside the saloons. "You could buy a drink any place in Las Vegas," recalled Harry Hall, a patron of Block 16. "We could buy a gallon of whiskey for $4 and it was pretty fair stuff."

One of the many reasons the sale of bootleg alcohol became so proficient was that local law enforcement looked the other way. Lawmen such as Sheriff Sam Gay and his deputy Joe Keate alerted local bootleggers of impending raids from the federal government. "Joe Keate would come out and give them the word when the federal marshals were going to show up," recalled Hall. While the police didn't levy any fines or make any arrests, some of them did keep their hands in the pot with an activity called Collection Day. "On Collection Day they'd go into the spots and say 'Well, it's payday.' [The saloons] would pay off a percentage of whatever the fine would be, depending on the business."

The sale of bootleg alcohol was so out in the open that the production extended past the narrow walls of the canyon. Tents and shacks sprang up at the entrance to what the locals had named Bootleg Canyon. Each tent sold, and many also produced, bootleg beer or whiskey. The place grew very popular and at one time had more than fifty makeshift saloons that sold or produced bootleg alcohol. Copying their Block 16 counterparts, tents were set up where girls could be accessed; however, unlike Block 16, the area was not regulated. Lawmen Bud Bodell reported on the conditions when he raided the area. "Stinkingest thing I ever saw; damn water was full of rats and snakes. Some of them had tents out back where their wives were working. At least down on the line they visited a doctor every week. Out on the highway they had nothing."

The seriousness of the area became much more apparent when the building of the dam started. It was next to impossible to keep the workers away from the bootleg alcohol so readily available and it was affecting the work. "I know of one of the top officials who got laid off the job for excessive drinking," recalled dam worker Elton Garrett. "He was a good executive but that was his filling."

The federal government could no longer ignore the problem and was forced to take action. Because the bootleggers were always notified about impending raids, federal marshals took a different approach. In May 1931 former real estate agent Ralph Aubry Kelly opened a saloon called Liberty's Last Stand. Kelly worked as an undercover agent, purchasing bootleg alcohol from local moonshiners.

The saloon was a front meant to trap the seller. The deliveries were staggered so that the seller could be arrested without others being notified. "They would come in at a certain time, and the federal men would take them in, place them under arrest, place them in the back room, and get ready for the next one," recalled Elbert Edwards. "In the meantime there were other federal men hitting every known speakeasy in the area. They just cleared the valley of moonshiners, of bootleggers, saloon keepers, everything."

While bootleg alcohol was dealt a blow, it wasn't fatal. The defiant moonshiners continued the production of alcohol, although on a lesser scale, until on, December 5, 1933, the United States passed the Twenty-first Amendment, which repealed the Eighteenth Amendment. With the production of alcohol legal again, there was no longer a need for the bootleggers, they quickly went out of business, and the canyon dried up. Bootleg Canyon held the name and the artifacts that can still be seen in the canyon to this day. The area, now owned by Boulder City, was turned into mountain bike trails. When these world-class trails were created, the trail groomers chose to leave the containers, smokestacks, mattresses, and even old cars in the area as part of the scenery and history of the Las Vegas residents who refused to follow the law.

EARLY MAN DISCOVERED
IN LAS VEGAS

1930

"Curiously enough, the thing that first aroused my interest in the exploration of Gypsum Cave in Southern Nevada was manure," recalled Mark R. Harrington. That interest eventually led to a scientific discovery attracting worldwide attention.

Located fifteen miles east of Las Vegas, the Gypsum Cave is nestled in the Frenchman Mountain Range. Harrington had been attracted to the cave by "vague rumors that it might hold something of architectural interest." On that January day in 1930, when he entered the dark, musty cave, Harrington found a thick layer of a hard dried fibrous substance. When Harrington spoke with the local residents about the cave, he was told that the substance was seaweed left over from a time when the cavern contained a subterranean lake. But Harrington had cleaned out far too many stables as a young man not to know that the substance on the floor of the cave was dried feces. The only question that remained in his mind was how it got there.

Mark Raymond Harrington was born July 6, 1882, on the campus of the University of Michigan. His father, a teacher at the university, was also curator of the school's museum. Even from an early age, Harrington had a fascination with Native American culture. In his adulthood he lived with many Native American tribes and bands in North America, writing stories based on his adventures under the pen name Raymond de la Cuevas (Raymond of the Caves).

Harrington worked with his father as an apprentice field archaeologist, eventually earning a master's degree in anthropology from Columbia University. He was highly skilled in both archaeology and ethnology, proving to have a remarkable ability to accurately date artifacts even before carbon dating was invented. He and a friend formed a business called Covert & Harrington, Commercial Ethnologists. They arranged exhibits of Native American artifacts at schools, colleges, and museums.

The entrance to the cave was small and Harrington had to squeeze himself in before pulling his tools behind him. He stayed at the entrance to best take advantage of the limited light. Removing a small shovel from his pack, Harrington dug into the ground covering. He knelt down, pulled up a sample, and examined it closely. When Harrington broke the sample apart he was able to clearly identify plant fibers. Based on his findings, Harrington determined that the animal that left the deposit had to have survived on a diet of plants; this meant it was an herbivore. Looking closely at the broken sample, Harrington further determined that the feces were most likely left by an animal living in prehistoric times. This sparked Harrington's interest. As the gears spun inside his brain, he made a mental list of animals that could have both lived in the area and been small enough to fit inside the low entrance of the cave. Harrington was discouraged when no matter how hard he tried, his list only contained carnivores, or meat eaters.

And then it came to him. The ground sloth, an Ice Age animal resembling a bear, fit the bill. Not only had it lived in the area, the size was right, and, best of all, it was an herbivore. Harrington sent a sample of the feces to the American Museum of Natural History and received a confirmation that Gypsum Cave had indeed been a den for ground sloths.

Excited at the confirmation of his findings, Harrington returned to the cave to conduct further exploration. Although the entrance was small, the inside of the cave opened to a large cavern. Harrington turned on his headlight and covered his mouth with a dust mask. Digging into the ground his excitement grew at the thought of what treasures he might find. He had been digging for only a short time when he lifted a small round shaft from under layers of dried feces. Cleaning it off, he noticed that it was broken. Harrington figured that other pieces of the shaft would be near and he had a good idea that what he had found was a dartshaft, an Ancient American weapon.

Digging further Harrington discovered several pieces of wooden dartshafts. Being an expert in Native American culture, Harrington dated the artifacts to a tribe living in the ancient Basketmaker period over two thousand years ago. Ancestors to the Paiute tribe who were currently living in the area, Basketmakers derived their name from the tightly woven baskets found in the remains of pit-houses in Southern Nevada. Harrington knew that the Basketmakers used the dartshafts as weapons and wondered if discovering a two-thousand-year-old weapon might lead to a discovery of an even older culture.

Harrington hurriedly formed an expedition and returned once again to the cave. One of the members, Bertha "Bertie" Parker Pallan functioned as secretary. Bertie came from a family of archaeologists, having been born in a tent during one of her father's many excavations. "Bertie comes naturally by her archaeological interest," Harrington wrote in an article. It was her custom to put on the headlight and dust mask and explore the cave when her work on the excavation was completed for the day.

One day after work Bertie began exploring a section called Room 3. This section hadn't been explored as much as the other areas and Bertie hoped it would lead to an exciting discovery. She had been digging in the ground for quite some time when she noticed a large flat slab. She moved over to the slab and positioned her head to take advantage of the light on her forehead. When she peered into the cave, she saw what looked like a bone. Her excitement grew as she wondered if she had discovered the remains of a Basketmaker. Bertie slid her arm into the crevice and took hold of the item. She slowly removed it, being careful not to drop or crush it. The process seemed to take hours, but when she finally pulled it from its hiding place she held in her hand a curious-looking skull. She immediately brought it to Harrington.

"When I saw it, I was tempted to shout 'Ground Sloth'," recalled Harrington, who sent the skull to the California Institute of Technology. Testing confirmed that the skull was in fact that of a ground sloth. The discovery was very instrumental to the excavation. Based on the finding of the skull alone, the California Institute of Technology and the Carnegie Institute of Washington joined the excavation, offering financial support.

Further diggings discovered remains of other animals, including two species of camels, llamas, and two types of Native American horses. Harrington continued digging where the skull was located and found a dartpoint "skillfully chipped of quartz." He also discovered fragments of wooden dartshafts that had been decorated with "bands, spirals, dots, little diamonds, and squares." These examples of early American art were made with colors of red, green, brown, and black.

But the most important discovery of all happened in Room 1. Harrington and his team had dug about eight feet below the surface when they found ashes and wood charcoal indicating a campfire. "This had been a camping place for aboriginal visitors to the cave," Harrington claimed. It also meant that humans had been in the cave earlier than first predicted. Harrington had gone looking for examples of Ice Age man and, based on these discoveries, he had found him.

Because of these findings, Harrington concluded that the Basketmakers had been in the caves at the same time as the sloths. This would mean that the Basketmakers were in the area at around 8,500 B.C., according to Harrington's estimates (he would later reduce that date to 7,500 B.C.). The excavation received national attention, mainly in the form of scientists and universities disputing Harrington's claims, while others defended them.

Radiometric tests would eventually date the sloth feces to the period of time between 9,700 and 6,500 B.C. Those same tests would date the human remains from 900 to 400 B.C., placing them at different time periods and disputing the findings made by Harrington. A 2004 expedition returned to Gypsum Cave and concluded that the layers of sloth feces were actually one layer. The expedition also concluded that the radiocarbon dates of the feces were consistent with the period of time when the sloth was known to have become extinct. The team further concluded that the ashes and wood charcoal were most likely residue from mold or decomposed sloth dung. As far as the dartpoints and dartshafts were concerned, the team attributed their positions in the cave to packrats that "had scurried through this three-dimensional natural maze, dragging their treasures through the deposits."

No matter what the final outcome, Harrington and his team made some very fine discoveries of human artifacts and animal remains. Many of these artifacts and remains, including sloth claws, were placed on display at the Southwest Museum in Los Angeles. When asked why he chose the life of an archaeologist, Harrington said, "To follow the trail of a forgotten people, to play detective upon the doings of a man who has been dead ten thousand years or so is a thrilling pastime to an explorer under any circumstances."

A TOWN PREPARES FOR THE DAM

1930

On December 30, 1930, President Calvin Coolidge authorized the building of a dam to contain the Colorado River and produce energy for the inhabitants of Nevada, California, and Arizona. It would be the catalyst that would spark a boom in the struggling town of Las Vegas.

By 1930 the population of Las Vegas had grown to more than five thousand. But Las Vegas had been struggling since the Union Pacific railroad pulled their repair shops out in 1922, forcing the town to find another source of commerce. Leaving with the railroad were hundreds of railroad employees. The loss of residents had a ripple effect on all business in the area. So when the director of reclamation services Arthur Powell Davis proposed a canyon near Las Vegas as the place to build a dam that would tame the Colorado River, the town took hope.

Rumors of a desire to control the Colorado River began as early as 1919. At the time, the mighty Colorado routinely ran its banks, flooding precious farming land and causing thousand of dollars worth of damage every year. Davis, nephew of explorer John Wesley Powell, headed up a search of over seventy locations to place the dam. After weighing the pros and cons of each site, Davis narrowed the choices to two canyons, both located a short distance outside of Las Vegas. In 1928 California congressmen Philip Swing and Hiram Johnson proposed a bill to build the dam. It was signed into law on December 21, 1928, and when it passed the tiny town of Las Vegas went wild. "We got the fire truck out," recalled Leon H. Rockwell, resident of Las Vegas. "Everybody that could hooked on to it! In carts and baby buggies and everything else—just like they was nuts."

When city officials found out the secretary of the interior Ray Lyman Wilbur was to visit in 1929, they were determined to show Las Vegas in the best light possible. Block 16, the area of town that had become famous for gambling, alcohol, and prostitution was closed. A banner proclaiming Las Vegas as "The Gateway to Boulder Dam" was erected across Fremont Street, the main street downtown. When Wilbur arrived he was given the grand tour and shown a Las Vegas eager for his business and that of his workers.

Unfortunately, Wilbur wasn't fooled by his visit and, unbeknownst to city officials, had already made the decision to construct a government town, called Boulder City, on land close to the construction site. Wilbur viewed Las Vegas as a dirty little town whose residents had only one concern—the pursuit of pleasure. Being a religious man, Wilbur was put off by Las Vegas's flagrant defiance of prohibition laws and its open promotion of prostitution. He would have none of that in his town. Wilbur intended to construct Boulder City with strict rules prohibiting the sale of alcohol, the practice of gambling, and of course, prostitution.

Las Vegas officials were initially put off by Wilbur's desire to rid his workers of the terrible influences that awaited them in Las Vegas. But after some thought, they reasoned that the strict rules imposed by Wilbur would entice workers to come to Las Vegas for rest and relaxation. They also knew that those visits would increase the town's revenue. The U.S. government was to spend almost $50 million on the dam and Las Vegas was poised to benefit from much of that money. The supplies needed to build and support the dam would have to be stored somewhere and that somewhere would be Las Vegas. In preparation, city officials planned the construction of forty new buildings.

The most ambitious project would come in the form of a road. "There was no paved highway between Las Vegas and Boulder City," recalled resident John Cahlan. "It was a dirt road and it was nothing more than just a place cleared out so the cars could drive." If Wilbur wouldn't let Las Vegas come to his workers, then city officials would make it easier for the workers to come to Las Vegas. In 1931, bonds were issued to widen, pave, and extend existing city streets. City officials seized the opportunity to include Fremont Street in the expansion plans. The bond raised $165,000. But city officials didn't stop there. They created a plan that would make Fremont Street a highway between Las Vegas and Boulder City. This plan allowed them to tap into government funds to build and expand the road.

While much of the country was struggling with the Great Depression, Las Vegas was booming. Many of the downtown properties spruced themselves up in anticipation of new clientele. Hotel Nevada added another floor with fifty new rooms. The new Apache Hotel boasted one hundred rooms and the town's first elevator. Even small hotels, such as the MacDonald, added sixteen new rooms.

Restaurants, like the Green Shack, were popular eating establishments for dam workers sick of cafeteria food, preferring Miss "Jimmie" Jones's homemade fried chicken. "The Green Shack was one of our favorite places to go for chicken," recalled Mary Ann Merrill, the wife of one of the workers. "A whole bunch of us would go into town. We'd order our chicken on our way in, and go downtown in Vegas. They'd have it in a big basket, and they had hot biscuits and gravy. Very good."

The valley also got an influx of people hoping to escape the Great Depression. Moving to the area without a pre-arranged job, these people hoped to get work at the dam. Instead, many ended up working in Las Vegas during the construction boom. The immigrants to the area set up camp on the shore of the Colorado River near the construction of the dam. A resident of the time, George L. Ullom, described the scene. "Everybody was coming. They were living in the bushes. There'd be two hundred people sleeping either on the ground or on the benches." The men brought their families and everything they owned. Because they lived in tents, the area would come to be known as "Ragtown."

Wilbur appointed Sims Ely as Boulder City manager. Ely governed the company town with an iron fist. In an article in the *New York Times,* a resident claimed "A feller couldn't make a real old-time western town out of Boulder City if he tried," complaining that the town officials were "only after jobs." This made Las Vegas the place to be when the work was done for the day. It also brought needed revenue to the town.

Las Vegas's gamble on the workers at the Boulder Dam paid off. "It was always fun to go to Vegas. We went to Vegas often," recalled Rose Lawson. The workers and the workers' wives would get away from what they called "the reservation" any time they could, especially to go shopping. "Las Vegas had Penny's and Ronzoni's," recalled Perle Garrett. "There were so many people who came there. You couldn't get anything unless you'd be right there."

Before residents of Boulder City could leave or get back on "the reservation" they had to stop at a gate and they had to have a pass. "We all had to have passes to go to Vegas," recalled Lawson. "Four miles out of [Boulder] city there was a gate." While the residents of Boulder City were allowed to come to Las Vegas—so long as they had their passes—Ely strictly controlled the goods flowing back into Boulder City. "What a time those poor reservation guards used to have," recalled Garrett. "You'd always have a lot of things in your car. They'd be out there in all that heat, going through every one of those packages, feeling, trying to find a bottle of liquor."

The downtown area was not the only part of Las Vegas experiencing growth. Homes started being built in the areas just south and east of the original townsite. A hospital was built on the corner of Eighth and Ogden. A high school, a theater, and two churches were also constructed. When the dam was finally completed, many of the workers left the reservation and settled in Las Vegas. "We had a population of around 7,000 in [Boulder City] while the dam construction was going on," recalled Boulder City resident Elton Garrett. "When the dam was finished, the population shrank to about 2,500." And while Boulder City survived, Las Vegas was only beginning the growth it would experience in the decades to come.

THE FIRST CASINOS

1931

In the back of the Northern Club, a group of men gathered around a table wearing apprehensive looks. Smoke filled the air. Sitting at the table were a city councilman, a state official, two assemblymen, a business booster, some club owners, and Lester Stocker, the organizer of the meeting. The year was 1930 and Lester was determined to change the gambling laws in the state of Nevada. The Northern Club was owned by Lester's mother, Mayme Stocker, who had opened the club in 1920 in the infamous Block 16. At the time only five games of chance were legal in Nevada, three of which were poker games—stud, draw, and lowball. The other two were bridge and a game called "five hundred." Lester wanted to change the way gambling was conducted in Las Vegas.

In the midst of Prohibition, the family was already involved in the production of bootleg alcohol. But Lester understood the role that gambling could play to attract business in an alcohol-free environment. So he gathered the group of men to discuss what could be done to get a bill passed legalizing gambling on a broader scope. "If

I had some money to spread around I could probably get it on," one of the men in the group told Lester.

Lester and his brother Harold approached several other business owners and told them their idea. Lester explained how Las Vegas needed a new flow of income to stay alive and convinced them that gambling was the way to go. He also told them that the only thing holding it up was money. The group managed to raise $10,000, which they gave to assemblyman Phil Tobin. "So they got the legislator from Winnemucca, Phil Tobin, to introduce it, and the fellow took the money," recalled Harold. "I don't know who he gave it to. I don't know if he gave it to anybody. But the bill passed." While he did introduce the bill, Tobin claimed that he only got three bottles of scotch in the deal.

On March 9, 1931, at 3:45 p.m., the Nevada State Legislature passed assembly bill #98 legalizing gambling in the state of Nevada by a vote of twenty-four to eleven. The bill legalized slot machines, gambling games, and gambling devices. It also mandated that a license must be issued to have such gambling and a fee be paid for that license. Shortly after the bill was passed, in 1931, the first gambling license in the state of Nevada was issued to Mayme Stocker for the Northern Club.

While gambling was now legal, it would take another ten years before the saloon would change into the modern casino. This transformation took place on April 3, 1941, when the El Rancho Las Vegas opened its doors. According to Las Vegas legend, businessman Tom Hull was traveling from California to Las Vegas in 1940 when his car suddenly became difficult to steer. He pulled over to the side of the road, got out, and found he had a flat tire. As Hull waited for assistance, he couldn't help but notice the number of cars that passed along Highway 91, the road from Los Angeles to Las Vegas. Hull's business was hotels and the numerous cars gave him an idea.

While the story may or may not be true, Hull did travel to Las Vegas. He was invited to meet two men, who themselves had an idea. James Cashman was a car dealer and member of the chamber of commerce. He and land developer Robert Griffith were looking for a way to make Las Vegas more of a resort destination. The men had done their research and found Hull, who owned a successful chain of resorts in California called El Rancho. Cashman and Griffith figured that if they could get Hull to open one of his resorts in downtown Las Vegas, it would change the face, and the reputation, of the town. So the men invited Hull to town with the thought of convincing him to expand his California chain in Las Vegas.

Since most legends have some basis in fact, it is most likely that Hull did have the flat and that seeing all the cars made the two men's proposal a very soft sell. Griffith and Cashman wanted to clean up the downtown area known as Block 16 and hoped that Hull's resort would do the trick. They showed Hull property along the developing Fremont Street near Block 16, but much to their surprise, Hull chose a spot along the Los Angeles Highway that, at the time, was far out of town. Of course, the fact that land was cheap, taxes were lower, and water rights were not questioned may have also played a part. So too did the fact that the town of Las Vegas levied a slot machine tax that did not exist in the county outside of the township.

No matter what spurred his interest, Hull bought thirty-three acres for $150 per acre from a woman who owned the land. The woman had considered the land useless and was happy to get rid of it. The property Hull purchased was located on the southwest corner of Highway 91 (now Las Vegas Boulevard) and San Francisco Street (now Sahara Avenue), just south of the spot where the Sahara Hotel and Casino is currently located. Cashman was very upset with Hull's choice. It didn't fit into his dreams at all and he was not happy. Although Hull's location was only three miles from

Fremont Street and the notorious Block 16, Cashman referred to the spot as the "boondocks."

Despite Cashman's concerns, Hull was undaunted. He built a sprawling Spanish mission–style complex complete with a casino, coffee shop, buffet, restaurant, showroom, pool, forty cottages—surrounded by lush gardens—and parking for four hundred vehicles. Hull also had a windmill built. He placed it on top of the main building and lit it up at night in bright neon. He wanted his resort to be seen even at night, and he used the windmill as a beacon to all traveling motorists.

While the El Rancho Las Vegas did have a casino, it was small even by 1941 standards, having only one craps table, two blackjack tables, and one roulette wheel. There were no poker tables and few slot machines. What the El Rancho did have was entertainment. Hull wanted his hotel to be a resort not a casino. So he brought in women from California, dressed them in what were considered revealing costumes for the times, and put them in a show. Hull's "El Rancho Starlets" were the first showgirls in Las Vegas. Hull also brought in big Hollywood names such as Milton Berle, Jackie Gleason, and Jimmy Durante to entertain and bring in crowds.

At the time of the El Rancho's opening, few people gave it much chance of success, being so far out of town. However, the opposite was true. While Hull would turn out to be a poor manager of casino resorts—he sold the property a year and a half after opening—he opened the door to the modern Las Vegas casino and started the trend to put resorts on what would eventually be called the Las Vegas Strip.

Shortly after the opening of the El Rancho another Griffith came to town. Originally from Texas, R. A. Griffith owned a chain of movie theaters in the Southwest. While some reports stated that this Griffith had been on his way to Deming, New Mexico, to open another theater, others stated that he was on his way to California from Deming where he had considered opening a chain of hotels. What is certain is that Griffith—no matter which direction he was traveling—stopped in Las Vegas and stayed at the El Rancho. And, upon seeing how successful Hull and the El Rancho were, he decided to compete.

Griffith approached the owner of a small club on thirty-five acres even further away from Las Vegas. Called the 91 Club (formerly the Pair-O-Dice), its owner was an ex–Los Angeles police captain named Guy McAfee who was willing to sell for the right price. That price turned out to be $1,000 an acre and came after much bargaining. Once the deal was closed, McAfee, check in hand, told Griffith "If you had bargained harder, I would've sold for less." Griffith responded with "If you had bargained harder, I would've paid more." When the deal was complete, McAfee carried the $35,000 check around for over a month. He showed the check to everyone he came in contact with and told them he had "caught a Texas sucker."

R. A. Griffith turned the thirty-five acres—located about a mile south of the El Rancho—into a resort called The Last Frontier, which opened on October 30, 1942. As the name suggests, the resort had a western theme. Its main building was designed to resemble a lodge. It had high ceilings and a fireplace that sat in the center, its chimney running right up through the roof. Griffith brought in Navajo workers from New Mexico who set stone from nearby Red Rocks. He also transferred the forty-foot mahogany Gay Nineties Bar from the famous Block 16 Arizona Club that had been closed. Bar stools were carved to look like saddles. Additional segments were added to the building and arranged to give the appearance of a street from an old western town.

The Last Frontier, like the El Rancho, had one-story hotel rooms, called bungalows. Griffith worried about the effect the Las

Vegas heat would have on his guests and the low room occupancy that might come as a result during the summer months. Working with his engineering staff, Griffith developed a method of dealing with the scorching heat. Tunnels were dug under the rooms and used to circulate cold water. The water was then passed through pipes installed in the walls of the rooms, keeping them cool. Griffith also planted 3,700 trees, plants, and shrubs to help to cool the property.

The Last Frontier was the first resort to offer what is now a Las Vegas staple. The Little Chapel of the West—often called The Hitching Post—was the first wedding chapel located in a Las Vegas resort. Made of redwood, the chapel was an exact replica of a church built in a California pioneer town.

The success of both the El Rancho and The Last Frontier launched a movement of businesses south. Wholesale and retail businesses, as well as roadside shopping centers and smaller motels, soon filled Highway 91 (later renamed Las Vegas Boulevard). The saloons on Fremont Street and Block 16 followed suit and transformed themselves into the resort-style hotels that stole business away from downtown Las Vegas.

While it changed the face of casinos and led the way to the modern Las Vegas resort, the El Rancho suffered a debilitating fire on June 16, 1960, and was never rebuilt. Suffering the fate of many Las Vegas landmarks, the El Rancho was imploded on October 3, 2000. The Last Frontier fared better, although it was sold many times and renamed the New Frontier. It was eventually closed on June 16, 2007. Five months later, on November 13 of that same year, the building was imploded to make way for a new project.

VEGAS HELPS THE WAR EFFORT

1941

High above the desert on a cold December day, a plane flew a steady, straight line. Behind it, another plane in tow moved erratically as the wind whipped through the thousands of holes in its fuselage. A third plane, a U.S. Army Air Corps B-17, followed the two, closing in at a fast pace. In no time at all the B-17 pulled up alongside the towed plane. A young man sitting in the B-17's gun turret looked through the sights of his machine gun and focused in on the helpless plane. He pulled the trigger and the gun came to life, littering the plane with hundreds more holes, lead piercing metal. The young man smiled and received a thumbs up from his trainer. He got out of the seat so another could take his place and the B-17 banked for another approach.

On the ground, at an indoor range, men took aim at rows of miniature, black-silhouetted planes. The planes traveled along set paths, in a type of arcade game. The young men fired upon the planes that when hit, just as in the arcade, fell over. These scenes, and many like them, were repeated thousands of times as the Air Corps Gunnery

School conducted its mission of "training of aerial gunners to the degree of proficiency that will qualify them for combat duty."

War raged in Europe as Adolf Hitler steadily expanded the German Empire. Las Vegas's tentative entry into the war effort began in 1940 as the U.S. government searched for a place to train the men who would handle the machine guns in their new B-17 bomber, called the "Flying Fortress," and the B-24 bomber, called the "Liberator." Las Vegas was a perfect choice. The weather allowed year-round training, and it was sparsely populated in 1940 with only about eight thousand people. This meant that planes flying over the large desert area posed little danger to the small community during training activities. Pleased with their choice, the Army Air Corps surveyed land just outside Las Vegas to place the school.

While the U.S. government surveyed land in Las Vegas, Nevada senator Patrick McCarran straightened his tie and prepared himself for a meeting with President Franklin D. Roosevelt. McCarran was intent on convincing Roosevelt that Nevada was the perfect place to mine the magnesium needed for bombs. Germany's relentless bombing of England made it difficult for a factory to be built in Europe, and magnesium was plentiful in the hills at Gabbs, Nevada, just three hundred miles north of Las Vegas.

McCarran presented his best case and convinced Roosevelt to mine magnesium in Nevada. In 1941 the U.S. government signed a contract with Basic Magnesium Inc. Once the contract was signed, the largest magnesium plant in the United States was constructed, employing fourteen thousand construction workers. While the magnesium was mined in Gabbs, the plant was located just outside of Las Vegas in the valley between Las Vegas and Boulder City. The location funneled thousands of federal dollars into the Las Vegas community.

Plans for the gunnery school were launched into high gear on December 7, 1941, when the Japanese bombed the Pearl Harbor

Naval Base in Hawaii. The bombing thrust the United States into World War II, pushing the Las Vegas Air Gunnery School into full swing. Only two days after the Pearl Harbor bombing, the chief of the Air Corps ordered training for aerial gunners to begin in Las Vegas. By the end of that year 320 students entered the Air Corps Gunnery School each week.

The training lasted five weeks. Students started with shotguns mounted to the backs of trucks. The trucks were driven through a course as students focused and fired on targets. While the weather allowed for year-round outdoor training, indoor ranges were also used to hone skills. The fighter-plane targets used in the arcade-type activity were scaled to represent ranges of two hundred, four hundred, and six hundred yards. The planes moved at approximately four hundred feet per minute and fell over when hit. Because live rounds were needed for the war, small round BBs were used in the machine guns instead of actual live rounds. The BBs also prevented the targets from being completely destroyed by live ammunition every time they were hit. Heavy fabric backings surrounded the range and absorbed the BBs. To keep the training steady, students were encouraged to use the range in their free time.

While the arcade-type of shooting worked well to hone reflexes, it did little to help the gunner shoot at the angles common to fighter planes as they banked into shooting range. To help with this type of training, a device was created that would better simulate these angles. The gunner was placed in a simulated plane, meant to represent the turret. A looped track was located a short distance in front of the plane. A flat paper target was mounted on a trolley that rotated around the track. The target was a 1:30 scale and was able to move around the track at speeds of two hundred, two hundred fifty, and three hundred miles per hour. Eventually two targets, going in opposite directions, were used.

The student was able to move the simulated plane, and thus the machine gun, as necessary to provide the proper lead angles to hit the target. The student's machine gun shot six hundred rounds per minute and each student was given one hundred rounds of BBs. The student's score was based on the percentage of successful shots, determined by the number of holes in the target.

In 1942 the first B-17 arrived on the newly formed base, exciting the students and sending the gunnery school into a new aspect of training. The school used fifteen thousand square miles of air space and forty-seven hundred square miles of land in their training. The dry lake beds in the area were perfect for emergency landings, while the rocky hills proved the right place for cannon and machine gun fire. The B-17s allowed the students to take their training to the skies in an environment that would more closely represent the conditions they would experience in actual combat.

On July 13, 1942, the Las Vegas Air Corps Gunnery School made the cover of *Life* magazine. A student sporting the official school t-shirt held one of the machine guns that were mounted on the bombers. By the end of 1942, 10,562 students had enrolled in the gunnery school with 85 percent of those students graduating. From 1942 to 1945 the gunnery school graduated approximately 600 gunnery students and 215 co-pilots every week, although some estimates placed that number at 4,000 total students per week.

By 1943 more than eight thousand servicemen were stationed at the base. The magnesium processing plant was also in full production. Completed in May 1943, the plant employed more than six thousand workers and produced more than 20 percent of the magnesium used in the war.

Toward the end of the war, the school tried a new training technique. The Air Corps was unhappy with the BBs used in training. Once in the field, the students found the guns that used BBs did not adequately represent the way an actual machine gun handled in combat situations. The school got rid of the BBs and instead used breakable ammunition in a program called "Operation Pinball." This new ammunition was fired at P-63 aircraft installed with a special armor. Instead of going through the target, the ceramic ammunition disintegrated when it contacted the target. A light in the propeller hub came on when a hit was scored. The program became so successful that all gunnery schools switched to the ceramic ammo by the end of the war.

The end of the war also brought the end of many of Las Vegas's war efforts. In 1944 Basic Magnesium Inc. closed down their processing plant, causing their nearly thirteen thousand employees to leave Las Vegas. After the surrender of Germany, the airfield served as a processing and separation center until it was closed in 1945. Fortunately the U.S. government had spent more than $25 million on the airfield and base and was unwilling to see that money go to waste. Therefore, in 1947, the airfield was reopened and used to train fighter pilots for the upcoming Korean War. In 1950 the base was renamed Nellis Air Force Base and is currently "Home to the Fighter Pilot."

BLOCK 16 COMES TO AN END

1942

On December 2, 1940, a group of squad cars rolled up in front of saloons filled to capacity with men and a few women. The faint sound of music drifted into the cool air as sixteen police officers, including the commissioner and chief of police, exited the cars and headed toward the front doors. When the police rushed in, the men and women inside were confused and taken by surprise. They were doing what they had done every night for years—dancing, drinking, and spending time with women.

Taking advantage of the situation, the policemen spread out, taking most, if not all, of the confused women into custody. The women protested, cursing the police and in some cases fighting with them. Chaos erupted. The music came to a grinding halt and most of the men scattered. Twenty-two women were removed from the saloons, or more appropriately brothels, taken to the police department and charged with prostitution. They were the first charges of their kind on the infamous Block 16 in thirty-six years, and it marked the beginning of the end of legalized prostitution in Las Vegas.

Block 16 was created in 1905 when William Clark plotted out lots of land for sale by auction. Clark set aside two plots, Blocks 16 and 17, as the only places where liquor could be sold without licensing restrictions. Once the sales at auction were complete, saloons and bars wasted no time opening, attracting male residents. To get ahead of their competitors, many saloons offered entertainment in the form of gambling, music, and dancing girls.

Western towns in the late seventeenth and early eighteenth centuries were notorious for fighting, drinking, and gambling. Saloons and gambling halls were a staple in most western towns and even the smallest of towns had these establishments, which served as a gathering place for the community. The local saloon functioned as a social center. It was often the only place where news of the community was told and food was served.

One of the most famous saloons of the time was the Arizona Club. It catered to the local repair yard workers and miners, but also to the travelers brought in by the newly formed San Pedro, Los Angeles & Salt Lake Railroad. The Arizona Club, unlike most of its competitors, was not a shack hurriedly slapped together with any boards available. It was a brick and mortar building with a beautifully decorated entrance, its name projecting from its concrete façade. Many other saloons followed the Arizona Club's lead. The Double O, the Arcade, the Gem, the Star Saloon, and the Red Onion Club all opened in the area. Block 16 became famous in the West as a place for gambling, drinking, and women.

Las Vegas, ever since its inception, has always been a town associated with vices, and where one vice exists, others are bound to gather. This was the case with Block 16. Starting around 1906 saloons began to add rooms at the back, called cribs, where girls were sold along with the gambling and alcohol. While not all of the saloons offered prostitution, enough did that the area became known for it. "Block

16 was where the girls were. They had a whole block of them there all on one side of the street, two blocks off of Fremont Street. They'd sit out front in the summertime and the spring of the year, and you'd drive by," recalled local resident Dean Pulsipher. "People would come to Vegas just to go to Block 16."

Saloons that offered prostitution were known as brothels. One of the brothels was even owned by the local sheriff. "The sheriff owned Roxies, which was the biggest place we had. It was very well organized and it was very well handled. We used to have them for customers and they were as much ladies as anyone else in town. They paid their bills, had their work done, and never any trouble," recalled local hairdresser and shop owner Joanne Imprescia.

Not all residents of Las Vegas supported prostitution. In fact, many vehemently opposed it. But their desperate cries went unheard and town officials decided to control the practice rather than fight it. The girls were even treated medically. "They had a health examination done by the city health officer. And I think it was a weekly checkup," recalled local resident Thomas Wilson. "It was controlled medically. They had to go to the hospitals—whatever the accommodations were in those days—it was very well done and very well supervised," recalled Imprescia.

Although the city controlled prostitution, the objections of the local residents did not go completely unheeded. "Block 16 was an isolated area and the ladies of the evening were not allowed to come up Fremont Street during any time of the week, except on Friday," recalled local attorney Herbert Jones. "They had to do all their business: go to the drugstore, get their cosmetics, and do all their purchases for their clothing and things of that nature on a Friday. Other than that they were restricted to what we called in those days Block 16."

Block 16 ran so well that even the police allowed the area to run on its own. "There was one gal down there by the name of Vera," recalled newspaper journalist John Cahlan. "She was queen of the block, and whatever she said went. She kept it under pretty good control, and no problems. If anything went wrong, the police would go down and tell Vera about it and she'd correct it."

But while vices may have been king in Las Vegas, even vices have to move out of the way when progress, or more importantly, profit take center stage. When secretary of the interior Ray Lyman Wilbur came to town in 1929, the brothels and saloons were shut down. According to Cahlan, "On the day scheduled for Wilbur's arrival in a private car, the word went out from the police department that all of the houses of prostitution on North First Street would be closed and there would be no liquor in the community until Wilbur got out of the city."

The reason the town covered its vices was because they were trying to show their best face. They wanted to attract the railroad and dam workers, which Wilbur, being in charge of the Bureau of Reclamation, had control over. But while Las Vegas was willing to hide its vices only temporarily for Wilbur, it wasn't able to do the same when an even bigger opportunity came along.

In October 1940 Army Air Corps vehicles rolled onto a piece of desert approximately thirty miles southwest of the growing town of Las Vegas. The air was cool and the wind still as a group of men, led by Major David M. Schlatter, got out of their government vehicles and set up expensive surveying equipment. The U.S. Army Air Corps, predecessor to the U.S. Air Force, was looking for a place to locate base facilities for an aerial gunnery school and the area outside the fast-growing town of Las Vegas proved to be an ideal spot.

When the United States armed forces showed interest in opening an airstrip in the little town, city leaders almost tripped over themselves to make the deal. But there was one major hurdle—Block 16. Schlatter met with city officials and told them that as long as Block

16 stood, no military personnel would be allowed to enter the town. Faced with a tremendous loss of profit, the city leaders ordered the 1940 raid and arrests.

The twenty-two women posted their $50 bail money and most of them simply returned to their brothels to continue business as usual. On January 25, 1941, city officials bought an airstrip and leased it to the Army Air Corps. A gunnery school and base was constructed on the site. While the raid allowed the deal to go through, the city still needed to rid itself of the offending vice. Elections were approaching and the residents against prostitution seized the opportunity and made the topic a hot issue. On January 2, 1942, with pressure from both the U.S. armed forces and the local community, city officials voted to cancel the gaming and liquor licenses for all of the establishments on Block 16.

With their main source of income gone, the saloons eventually closed down, though not all residents were happy with the decision of the city. One in particular recalled: "It got voted out and it's never been since and I think it's a mistake." Whether mistake or not, the brothels closed and the saloons were eventually demolished in 1946. The area where they once stood became the parking lots behind the California Hotel and Binion's Casino.

THE MOB COMES TO TOWN

1945

On the evening of June 20, 1947, police responded to a bungalow in the Hollywood hills. When they entered the home a gruesome sight awaited them. A man dressed in a $300 suit lay slumped on a flowered couch, hands in lap. Had it not been for the blood leaching from the man's eye socket, staining the front of his suit, the police might have thought he was simply asleep. Unfortunately, the rest this man was experiencing was eternal. Bugsy Siegel had been murdered in his California home.

Many tales of Las Vegas give the renowned mobster known as Bugsy Siegel credit for inventing the small town. The truth is, Las Vegas was already invented and growing when Siegel decided to build his dream resort. It already boasted many successful downtown casinos, two thriving resort casinos—the El Rancho and The Last Frontier—and many other businesses along the growing Highway 91 (later renamed Las Vegas Boulevard).

Benjamin "Bugsy" Siegel was born in Brooklyn, New York, on February 28, 1906, to Jewish immigrants. A juvenile delinquent from an early age, Siegel quickly worked his way into the hierarchy of the criminal underworld. Because he had a reputation for erratic behavior, Siegel was given the nickname "Bugsy," as in "crazy as a bedbug," a common term at the time. Siegel hated the name. "My friends call me Ben, strangers call me Mr. Siegel, and guys I don't like call me Bugsy, but not to my face." Siegel also had a very noted temper. When he was mad his voice would get very soft and, according to his attorney Greg Bautzer, "His blue eyes would turn a slate gray color."

Siegel had risen up the ranks far enough to be good friends with Mob bosses Meyer Lansky and Charles "Lucky" Luciano, who had together opened a series of illegal casinos and speakeasies all along the eastern shore in the 1920s and '30s. The organization the two created became known as the syndicate.

While the two had always avoided expanding into Las Vegas because of the heat, when gambling was legalized in 1931, Lansky and Luciano took notice. They worked their way into three Fremont Street properties, using men with no records as fronts for the operations. They kept the weight of their hands in the business relatively quiet until 1941 when they decided to get more involved with the racing and sports betting operations in the downtown Las Vegas casinos. Siegel was sent to Las Vegas, along with Moe Sedway, to investigate.

Siegel helped the syndicate take a greater control over the race and sports book aspects, until they had a complete monopoly. While the smaller casinos complained of Mob involvement—even bringing those complaints to Carson City—the state, as well as the country, was more involved in the war efforts than in organized crime. This opened a door for the Mob, one that they gladly stepped through.

Siegel had been to Las Vegas on several occasions. He was fascinated with the film industry and wanted to be a Hollywood star. Siegel routinely stopped in Las Vegas on his many trips to California, were he fed his fascination with Hollywood. Siegel acted the part of a gentleman. Considered rather attractive, he surrounded himself with luxury. "I've never met a more courtly, a more gentlemanly man in my life," recalled singer Kay Starr. "I thought to myself 'Well if this is a gangster, I'd like to know more of them.'" Siegel even dated an actress, Virginia Hill, although it didn't stop him from chasing other interests.

When Siegel arrived in town, one of the first things he did was check out the casinos in the downtown and outlying areas. He quickly decided that he didn't like the atmosphere in the smaller, less sophisticated downtown properties. Instead, he preferred the outlying resorts, El Rancho and The Last Frontier. He stayed there so many times that he began to get an idea of opening one of his own.

Siegel had been under investigation by the Federal Bureau of Investigation (FBI) for many years, yet he had always managed to escape conviction on any count. Although some would claim that Siegel opened his resort in an attempt to make a transition to legitimate business, Siegel was a sociopath, and it is more likely that he simply saw the resort as a way to move Mob operations closer to his beloved Hollywood. To his credit, Siegel had a vision of taking the Las Vegas resort to the next step. In an attempt to emulate the resorts he stayed at in California, Siegel wanted his resort to be a posh, luxurious place where the Hollywood elite would come to play.

By 1945 Siegel had managed to raise $1 million toward the building of his new Flamingo Club—it was later changed to Flamingo Hotel for licensing purposes. Siegel was able to convince Lansky to allow him to build the resort. He found a property out on Highway 91 that was already struggling. Billy Wilkerson, a known gambler, had put more money than he could afford into a resort that he wasn't able to finish. Siegel came on board and quickly took over the project.

Unfortunately, Siegel had no idea how to build a resort and materials were hard to come by in the post-war era. Undaunted, the resourceful Siegel persuaded his Hollywood friends to supply materials used on the sets of their movies. But his constant changes in plans, such as insisting that each room have its own sewer system, quickly put him over budget and greatly behind schedule. There was also the rumor that materials would be stolen at night, only to be sold back to Siegel the next day. All of these problems combined to quickly turn Siegel's original $1 million into $6.5 million, most of which was provided by the syndicate.

Mob influence was growing in the downtown casinos. The Northern Club, once family owned, was now completely run by Moe Sedway. Other clubs were simply fronts for organized crime and those clubs were showing heavy profits. Unfortunately, unknown to Siegel, the syndicate—used to seeing immediate results on their investments—was very unhappy with the amount of money they had shuffled into the resort. The bosses held a meeting in Havana, Cuba, the day before the opening of the Flamingo. If the Flamingo turned out to be a success, Siegel would be given a chance to pay back the loan. If not he would be eliminated.

The resort finally opened on December 26, 1946. It had a health club, pool, tennis courts and golf course, shops, showrooms, and stables for forty horses. All of the 105 rooms had oversized beds and the casino reeked of luxury. But Siegel couldn't have chosen a more terrible day to open a resort. Although a desert, Las Vegas is still cold in the winter and it was worse in wet, rainy California. Weather conditions prevented many of Siegel's Hollywood connections from being able to make the trip. Also, because of the many delays, the rooms were not completed on time and many of the guests that did attend were forced to take rooms in the El Rancho and The Last Frontier. Losses were so heavy that after two weeks, Siegel, unable to pay his staff, was forced to close the doors.

While the casino reopened a short three months later, on March 1, 1947, and proved very successful, the decision had already been made and Siegel's fate was sealed. Lucky Luciano stated in his memoirs: "There was no doubt in Meyer's mind that Bugsy had skimmed this dough from his building budget, and he was sure that Siegel was preparing to skip as well as skim, in case the roof was gonna fall in on him."

Almost immediately after Siegel was murdered, three men walked into the Flamingo and took over operations. Gus Greenbaum took charge and under his guidance the fabulous Flamingo Hotel was exceptionally profitable, so much so that organized crime began to take a different look at the possibilities that awaited them in the desert city.

The Mob took to running casinos like rats to cheese. They understood the importance of making their clients happy and having some of the most well-known names as entertainment. Little by little the Mafia opened hotels along what was now being called "the Strip." In no time the Desert Inn, Aladdin, Sahara, Riviera, Dunes, Stardust, Tropicana, and the Sands all opened, many of which had ties to organized crime.

By the 1950s Chicago families had joined the New York syndicate in Las Vegas. Worried about growth adversely affecting the operations, the families met and hammered out a plan that would allow each to govern their own areas without conflict. The plan worked very well for a while and the residents of Las Vegas were not opposed to the presence of the Mob. In fact many took comfort in it. "I wasn't afraid and I felt very safe," recalled Virginia James, a Sands Texas Copa Girl. Actress Debbie Reynolds recalled, "No one got killed that wasn't supposed to and we were never frightened of anything of that sort." It appeared to the residents that while the desert outside of Las Vegas might be filling with bodies, the Mafia managed to keep crime to a minimum in the growing town.

By the late '60s the Mob had skimmed almost every bit of profit from the casinos. Vegas, as it is prone to do, was ready to change its image and the love affair with the Mob had come to a quick end. When Howard Hughes came to town in 1966, he was seen as a godsend. Many doors were opened and red tape cut to allow Hughes to purchase many of the casinos owned by the Mob. However, it wasn't until the mid '80s that corporations eventually pushed the Mob out of town for good.

While Siegel didn't live long enough to see his vision come true, his influence has had a lasting effect on Las Vegas, both in changing the face of the modern resort and ushering in the era of organized crime. His Flamingo remains one of the few hotel casinos that still exists on the space where it was originally built. It has resisted implosions and managed to change with the times. Although initially it may have had to close due to poor planning, once reopened, it has remained so for more than sixty years and Siegel, despite being in town for such a short time, has remained as strong an influence on Las Vegas as Elvis Presley, Wayne Newton, and Steve Wynn.

A MUSHROOM-SHAPED CLOUD
IN THE DISTANCE

1951

On a cold January morning in 1951, a team of scientists stood behind a metal bunker more than twenty miles outside of Las Vegas. Anticipation was high as the monotone voice droned out the numbers . . . "ten . . . nine . . . eight." While the scientists had an idea of what would happen when the voice reached "one," as they put on their goggles and peered through the opening in the bunker, none of them really knew for certain. When the voice finally reached one, time seemed to stand still.

A flash filled the bunker with a light as bright as the burning sun. The ground jumped in the distance, lifting large masses of dirt and fine dust into the air. As the cloud grew larger it formed into a giant mushroom. The scientists tried to adjust their senses. They heard a roar growing in the distance. The roar increased, getting louder, and the only thing the scientists knew for sure was that something was approaching . . . and it was approaching quickly.

As anticipation of the unknown grew to an almost overwhelming state, the scientists were hit by the force of a shockwave that smashed into them like a freight train. A couple of scientists were knocked to the floor. The rush of air, accompanied by an almost deafening sound, passed as quickly as it hit. The first atomic explosion at the Nevada Test Site was now part of history.

The rush to test the first nuclear weapon had started years earlier when Nikita Khrushchev exclaimed, during a diplomatic reception at the Kremlin, "Whether you like it or not, history is on our side. We will bury you." Khrushchev was feeling very confident that day. He knew that Russia had gotten ahold of plans for a nuclear weapon from traitors to the United States. Russia would turn those plans into the creation of a nuclear device, with the first test occurring in 1949.

World War II had come to an end just four short years earlier. At the time, the United States had only two nuclear weapons. They had dropped both of them on Japan to end the war. Earlier the United States had entered the nuclear era when President Franklin D. Roosevelt received a letter signed by Albert Einstein encouraging him to develop a nuclear weapon. While Einstein was a known pacifist, he was concerned that the Germans, who had invaded Czechoslovakia, would develop the weapon first, a weapon they wouldn't be afraid to use. What Einstein didn't anticipate was that the United States would not only develop the weapon, but also wouldn't be afraid to use it.

When Harry S. Truman became president in 1945, he took Khrushchev's threat seriously and the search for a site to test nuclear weapons began. Before Khrushchev's proclamation, nuclear weapons had already been tested by the United States in the South Pacific; however, now Truman wanted to bring the testing closer to home. He wanted it to take place in North America. He established the Atomic Energy Commission (AEC) to begin the search for a testing site. The areas of northern Canada and Alaska were first examined because they would have the least impact on population. But concerns about water contamination scrapped those choices almost immediately.

The search was narrowed to the south central Atlantic Coast and the arid Southwest based on the following criteria: accessibility to Los Alamos testing center in New Mexico, good communications, adequate radiological safety, reasonably regular topography, prospects of economy of preparation and operation, and avoiding undue public radiological hazard. Based on the established criteria, the candidates selected were the Las Vegas Bombing and Gunnery Range, the Dugway Proving Ground in Utah, the White Sands Proving Ground in New Mexico, and Camp Lejeune in Northern California.

After a close examination of all available sites, Truman signed an order, on December 18, 1950, making the Las Vegas Bombing and Gunnery Range the official site. Las Vegas was chosen because the mountain range "offered the greatest degree of safety from radiological hazards." The order was kept secret for reasons of national security. Quietly groups of government workers came to Las Vegas on a regular basis. They checked in at a local hotel and disappeared into the desert. Their secret mission did not stay secret for long.

On January 27, 1951, the United States tested their first nuclear weapon at the area eventually named the Nevada Test Site. Despite the government's best efforts to keep the testing a secret, word got out. When the *Las Vegas Review-Journal* published an article on the mushroom-shaped cloud in the distance, the Atomic Energy Commission assumed there was a leak in their organization. To find out, they sent the Federal Bureau of Investigation (FBI) to investigate the newspaper.

There was no leak. Despite the best efforts of the Atomic Energy Commission, it was impossible to control everything. "They could not control traffic," recalled *Review-Journal* editor John F. Cahlan. The traffic from California to Las Vegas was notoriously heavy and a truck driver coming down the hill toward Stateline, Nevada, saw the explosion. "He got into Jean and he very nicely called the *Review-Journal*, and we got an eyewitness account of the blast," said Cahlan.

The fact is, the scientists made the newspaper's work easy. While the scientists were very good at making nuclear weapons, they were not so good at covering their tracks. Every time they came to town they all checked into The Last Frontier Hotel and left 2:00 a.m. wake-up calls. Activity also increased at Nellis Air Force Base. That activity coincided with the Frontier check-ins. But the biggest clue of all was the bright light of the blast that could be seen as far away as San Francisco and Los Angeles. The FBI had a hard time believing that a conspiracy wasn't occurring, so Cahlan made up a story to tell them. "We've got a bellhop at the Last Frontier that calls us and tells us there have been calls left for two or three in the morning. So we are able to pinpoint the shots, at least the day that they were set off."

The word was out and Las Vegans took to the testing like a lizard to a hot rock. A spot on Mount Charleston between Lee and Kyle Canyons provided a perfect view of the blasts. Groups of people traveled to the top of the mountain early in the morning to view the explosions that occurred sixty-five miles away. The government, in an ambitious move, decided not to hide the blasts from the public. In April 1952 they established a vantage point, called "News Nob," on a rocky cliff that overlooked the site. News dignitaries including Cahlan, Walter Cronkite, and Bob Considine of the *New York Times,* were invited to view the blasts from News Nob.

Las Vegas quickly adapted to the nuclear age. The test site broadcasted public radio notifications of scheduled tests, warning people not to be in high places, such as ladders, during the tests. Blasts were commonplace. "The people in the casinos would be gambling and so forth, and they'd see the big flash of light," recalled Cahlan. When the flash was over they'd return to their games saying "well, there goes another one."

On November 12, 1951, Las Vegas made the cover of *Life* magazine with a photo of an atomic cloud visible behind the neon signs of the Pioneer and Las Vegas Clubs. The resourceful executives of the Pioneer Club turned the photograph into a postcard. The Desert Inn followed by making its own mushroom cloud postcard. Vegas enjoyed the attention. The atomic testing brought in business and that brought in money. The Las Vegas Chamber of Commerce issued press releases describing the testing grounds as just one of the many attractions Las Vegas had to offer.

The chamber produced a calendar of scheduled blasts for tourists. Hotels organized picnics to view the blasts, bakeries created mushroom-cloud cupcakes, and restaurants added atomic burgers to their menus. The Sands Hotel and Casino even offered an Atomic Cocktail. The residents also got involved in the action. Local hairdressers created atomic hairdos and Las Vegas High School put a mushroom cloud on the cover of their yearbook, the Wildcat Echo. JCPenney, which donated mannequins for experimental testing, published before and after photos of their mannequins in the local paper, in an attempt to get residents involved in civil defense.

But probably the most memorable tribute to the atomic era came in the form of a woman covered in a cotton frontpiece shaped like a mushroom cloud. While many hotels would crown one of their showgirls Miss A-bomb or Miss Atomic Bomb, the Sands Hotel Casino actually held a competition crowning Miss Atomic Bomb of 1957. Copa Room showgirl Lee Merlin, a blonde-haired beauty, became an enduring symbol of the era with nothing more than outstretched arms and a mushroom-shaped cotton cloud covering her midsection. Between 1951 and 1992 when full scale nuclear testing was placed on an indefinite hold, 928 tests were performed; 100 of those tests were above ground.

A FIVE-MONTH SHOWDOWN

1951

Two men, one older and one younger, sat at opposite ends of a felt-lined table. Another sat between them sporting a visor and dressed in a white shirt with bellowed sleeves, a garter tight around his arm. He was holding tightly onto a deck of cards. A large crowd had gathered to watch the two men.

The older man removed cards from his hand and placed them face down on the table. Whispers almost immediately rose from the crowd. In a heavy Greek accent he told the dealer how many new cards he wanted. The stack of chips in front of him was not half as large as that of his younger opponent. The veteran kept his tired gaze casual, not looking directly at the younger man, but not avoiding him either. The crowd quieted. The dealer pulled the cards from the deck and slid them across the table. The older man accepted the cards, took a quick glance, then placed them with the others on the table in front of him. The dealer turned to the younger man and waited.

The younger man repeated the actions of the veteran. He ordered a single card from the dealer with a slow Texas drawl. The younger man took the card from the dealer, looked at it, and resisted the temptation to smile. The older man pushed a stack of chips to the center of the table, increasing the already large pile. The action caused the crowd to take a collective breath in anticipation. The younger man paused briefly before pushing his own stack of chips into the center. He called his opponent's bet and then, as the crowd readied to breathe, pushed in another stack, and raised the bet.

The table the two men played at was located at the front entrance to Binion's Horseshoe, a casino in the downtown area of Las Vegas. The game had been going on for five months and the only things that changed were the dealers, the stacks of chips, and the men's clothes.

In the summer of 1949, a gambler by the name of Nick "The Greek" Dandolos approached casino owner Benny Binion with an idea. He wanted to challenge the best poker players in the world to a marathon game. Dandolos earned his nickname by being born in Rethymnon on the island of Crete. His family was wealthy and he went to school at the prestigious Greek Evangelical College, studying philosophy.

In 1901 at the age of eighteen he was sent to America by his father and given an allowance of $150 a week. Seen as a rite of passage, the trip to America was meant as a learning experience. Dandolos landed in Chicago, where he immediately got into gambling. Almost from the beginning Dandolos showed a knack for the game. His strong mind enabled him to judge percentages and odds. After a brief stint in Canada, Dandolos came back to America more than a half a million ahead. When he moved back to Chicago he discovered poker and craps. Playing against professionals, it took him no time at all to lose the half million.

While he may have lost a small fortune, Dandolos gained a much better prize—knowledge. He used that knowledge to play the game and managed to garner quite a reputation in the Windy City. He was offered jobs in many of the gambling halls, whose frustrated managers found it cheaper to pay him than to let him play. As with any dedicated gambler, Dandolos had won and lost large amounts of money over and over again. In one story Dandolos lost $1.6 million in a twelve-day craps game. In another he took a player for $150,000 and then offered to play double or nothing on one turn of the card, telling his opponent "let's see how much of a gambler you really are." His opponent declined. Whether any of these stories are true is a matter for debate. What is not debatable is the fact that in his forty years on the East Coast, Dandolos made quite a name for himself as a respected high stakes gambler. When he approached Benny Binion that summer in 1949, it was not an accident.

Benny "The Cowboy" Binion was a well-known figure in Las Vegas. Originally from Texas, Binion found school boring and preferred to spend time with his father, which is where he mastered the art of horse trading. Living in the campgrounds where the traders gathered in the early 1900s, Benny also learned the art of gambling, or more appropriately, the art of cheating. "Everybody had his little way of doing something to the cards," recalled Binion. "I wasn't too long on wising up to that. Some of them had different ways of marking them, crimping them." While Binion claimed that he never got involved in cheating, he also stated that he "was always pretty capable about keeping from getting cheated" as well.

After making money in bootleg alcohol, Binion began running illegal crap games in the 1930s. "If we had half an hour's notice we were going to be raided, we could clear it out," he recalled. Binion had brushes with the law and was even reported to have killed a man or two in his time. He eventually made his way to Las Vegas where in 1951 he opened a club on Fremont Street called Binion's Horseshoe.

Binion was, in his own way, ahead of the times. He was the first to place carpet in a downtown casino, the first to provide limousines to pick up guests, and the first to offer free drinks to gamblers. He was also the first to comp the little player. He would often say "If you want to get rich, make little people feel like big people." But his biggest innovation was raising the stakes on the table games. In a time when most casinos placed $50 limits on players, Binion raised his limits to $500. His theory was that professional gamblers, who tended to double their bets when they won, would be more tempted to bet more money and, therefore, lose more often. With the odds in the favor of the house, Binion played those odds, gambling that he would win more than he lost. He was right.

Binion's willingness to pave his own way made him the perfect choice for Dandolos to approach. He went to Binion's casino and pitched his idea. Binion liked the idea but had only one stipulation—that the game be played at the front entrance of his casino by a large window so that the public could watch. He also had a twist on Dandolo's original idea. Instead of holding a tournament with multiple players, Binion wanted to pit the two best players in the world against each other. So he talked Dandolos into playing only one person, a respected gambler named Johnny Moss whom Binion claimed was the best player in the world.

A fellow Texan, Johnny Moss was raised in Odessa. Moss had worked in saloons and pool halls as a young teen. Like Binion, he had learned the tricks of the trade from an early age. He also believed cheating to be wrong and never used the tricks he learned against other players. Instead, he was hired by many saloons to spot cheaters and keep the games honest. However, like most gamblers of those days he had to go on the road to make a living and the road was a dangerous place.

To protect themselves and their interests, most gamblers carried a pistol, and Moss was no exception. Once while playing in a small town, Moss noticed a hole in the ceiling and an eye poking through. Moss pulled out his gun and said "Now, fellas, do I have to go and shoot a bullet in the ceiling? Or are you going to send your boy down without any harm?" The men called Moss's bluff so he shot several rounds into the ceiling, wounding the peeper.

Binion called Moss and told him of the winner take all event while Moss was playing in Texas. Moss liked the idea and flew to Las Vegas. Binion publicized the game as a match of giants. One reporter compared it to King Kong fighting Godzilla. The first game started in January 1951; the last game would be played in May that same year. Reports of the buy-in the two players paid vary between $2 million and $4 million.

Moss was fifteen years younger than Dandolos and heavily favored to win. While both were experts in their fields, the two men couldn't have been more different. Dandolos was fifty-seven years old and used to playing big games with big players. He was a very social man who was also very articulate. Moss on the other hand was used to playing private big-stake games. He had little education and was very standoffish, but also very calculating.

The two players started with five-card stud but would eventually switch among many different games to keep the play interesting. They continued play day and night, exchanging pots between them. They stopped only for bathroom breaks and a few hours each night to sleep. Most gamblers admit that poker is 90 percent mental. While Dandolos had a reputation for playing days on end without sleep, the long days and brief breaks took their toll on both combatants, but more so on Dandolos.

As the final hand approached, Dandolos was showing obvious signs of exhaustion. The crowd was almost completely silent when he pushed his final stack of chips into the mix and called the bet. The dealer asked the two men to show their hands and an audible inhale of breath could be heard as the men flipped their cards to reveal their hands. Dandolos eyed the two hands and slowly rose to a standing position. He looked at Moss and bowed, after which he admitted his defeat saying "Mr. Moss, I have to let you go." He then left the table, went to his room, and slept.

Moss won the entire pot of what was booked as "The Biggest Game in Town." Binion stated that the public gathered each day to watch the event with the "fervor of dedicated sports fans." The game has been credited as the start of the World Series of Poker, which Binion brought to the Horseshoe in 1970 and is now televised around the world.

THE KING BOMBS

1956

When the Atomic-Powered Singer stepped on stage, the audience didn't know exactly what to expect. Before them stood a young man dressed in a respectable two-piece suit. He had a wooden guitar strapped around his neck and his hair, styled in a large pompadour, bobbed as he shuffled to the microphone. They had come that night to see their favorite comedian, Shecky Greene, but before he came on stage, they would have to endure the opening act. The audience, dressed in formal attire, clapped politely at the young man's entrance. He came on stage, thanked the audience, and launched into song. As the music always did, it ran through the young entertainer like a wave, moving his body in its wake. He wiggled and waggled and at one point bent his knees as he lifted himself onto his toes. The audience was shocked. The young entertainer known as Elvis Presley had bombed.

Elvis had been booked as the "Atomic-Powered Singer" in an attempt to cash in on Las Vegas's fascination with the nuclear testing that was filling their skies with mushroom clouds. And while the crowd politely applauded, it was clear they didn't understand Elvis.

Drummer D. J. Fontana recalled: "I don't think the people there were ready for Elvis. We tried everything we knew. Usually Elvis could get them on his side. It didn't work that time." While Elvis gave the same performance that sent crowds screaming all across America, in Las Vegas he was nothing like the entertainers these audiences were used to, like Shecky Greene, Jimmy Durante, and Red Buttons.

After the first show, which occurred on April 23, 1956, *Las Vegas Sun* reporter Bill Willard wrote: "For the teen-agers, the long, tall Memphis lad is a whiz; for the average Vegas spender or showgoer, a bore. His musical sound with a combo of three is uncouth, matching to a great extent the lyric content of his nonsensical songs." *Newsweek* would compare his Vegas debut to "a jug of corn liquor at a champagne party."

Of course Elvis wasn't entirely unknown. The teens of America had already discovered him, and he held four spots on Billboard's top ten that year. His agent, Colonel Tom Parker, was wise enough to schedule a Saturday matinee especially for teen fans. The matinee sold out, and Elvis played to a more enthusiastic crowd of screaming fans.

Not all of the people who went to the show came away unimpressed. Las Vegas resident Ed Jameson wrote a rebuttal to Willard. "He's not a Rock 'n' Roller nor is he a cowboy singer. He is something new coming over the horizon all by himself and he deserves his ever growing audience." Jameson was so impressed that he implored parents to take their children to hear the young entertainer. "Nobody should miss him. It would be a good way to get to know your own kids."

Elvis was not used to the reactions he received in Las Vegas and was eager to leave. He felt a little better when he learned that he had been able to gather some fans. An up and coming piano player and entertainer named Liberace came to see him one night. When the show was over, Liberace went backstage with his brother George and took some publicity photos. One photo showed Liberace with a guitar while Elvis stroked the keys of a piano. Although the two entertainers enjoyed each other's company, neither had any idea of the impact they would both have on the Las Vegas culture.

Elvis managed to finish out the two-week stint, which consisted of two twelve-minute shows a night. And while he didn't gather many fans, he did walk away with a hit song. Elvis and his band always hung out together. They were a close-knit group that enjoyed each other's company. Not impressed with gambling, the group could usually be seen at the pool where they either lounged or engaged in harmless horseplay. At night they went out on the town. One night they decided to check out the competing shows. They made their way to the Sands, which had opened four years earlier and had gained quite the reputation as the place to be in Las Vegas. The lounge act was Freddie Bell and the Bell Boys, and they sang a song called "Hound Dog." From the first time Elvis heard this song he was hooked. He went back over and over again until he learned the chords and lyrics. Two months later he played the song on Milton Berle's television show and "Hound Dog" became his next hit.

While Elvis's popularity grew, his debut in Las Vegas was quickly forgotten. The 1960s had come to town and brought with it the Rat Pack, a group of performers led by Frank Sinatra who made Las Vegas and the Sands Hotel and Casino their home. While the Rat Pack owned the 1960s, Las Vegas still had another opportunity to embrace its icon.

Already a household name, in 1964, Elvis was at the height of his movie career. That year he made a movie with starlet Ann-Margret called *Viva Las Vegas*. The movie was promoted with the slogan "It's that go-go guy and that bye-bye gal in the fun capital of the world." Elvis was more than a little apprehensive about returning to the town that rejected him. But his good looks and singing combined with Ann-Margret's tight pants and sweaters brought in hordes of moviegoers, both male and female. It, like all of Elvis's movies, was a huge success and started the town on its love affair with the King of Rock and Roll.

Elvis returned to the town in 1967, but not to perform. Instead, he was there to attend a wedding. While he had already been at a Vegas wedding with Ann-Margret in *Viva Las Vegas,* this time Elvis was marrying for real. On May 1, 1967, Elvis Presley and Priscilla Beaulieu were married at the Aladdin Hotel. It was an event that foreshadowed Las Vegas's link to Elvis.

Shortly after the release of *Viva Las Vegas,* Elvis's popularity had taken a bit of a hit when four lads from Liverpool started the British invasion of America. Four years later Elvis, clad in tight black leather, did a television show called "Comeback 68" that launched him back into the spotlight.

While Elvis was back at the top of his game, he still had one last obstacle to tackle. Bombing in Vegas hadn't sat well with him all those years, and he was determined to conquer the town that rejected him all those years ago. In 1969, Elvis signed on for a four-week stint with the International (later called the Las Vegas Hilton). As the show approached, Elvis became increasingly nervous. Probably recalling his first show in Sin City, Elvis wasn't even sure anyone would come out to see him. He was wrong. Elvis did two shows a night and set Las Vegas attendance records, selling out the 2,200-seat showroom every night. He also set a record for gross receipts with more than $1.5 million of revenue.

In 1969 Elvis performed in a dark black suit. By 1970 he had switched to what became his trademark one-piece jumpsuit—open to reveal his chest. His signature hairstyle now included long sideburns and he routinely wore thick gold-rimmed sunglasses. He also took to performing the martial arts moves on stage he had learned in private lessons. Elvis played Las Vegas every year for the next eight years, ending his run on December 12, 1976. He died less than eight months later.

Once Vegas accepted him it refused to let him go. While Elvis may have lived in Memphis, the residents of Vegas always considered him their hometown hero. On September 8, 1978, the King's first birthday after his death, the Las Vegas Hilton dedicated a bronze statue created by sculptor Carl Romanelli. The statue was placed in a glass case outside the showroom where Elvis performed.

To generate business, many hotels advertised "Elvis slept here" on their billboards. Of course he didn't sleep in any of those locations, but that didn't stop them from claiming it was true. Vegas turned into the home of the Elvis impersonators, with many lounge acts imitating the singer, even while his show was still running at the Las Vegas Hilton. Most of the impersonators dressed as Elvis in the 1970s, complete with gaudy jumpsuits, long sideburns, and big sunglasses. Stores even sold fake Elvis hairpieces and large lens, gold-framed sunglasses. A troop of skydivers formed, calling themselves the Flying Elvi. The group performed their aerial acrobatics dressed in jumpsuits, fake hair, and gold glasses.

But the local wedding chapels were the biggest part of Las Vegas to embrace the King. It became a big deal to have an Elvis impersonator sing "Love Me Tender" during the wedding ceremony. Some chapels even became Elvis themed. Lucky couples got married by a 1950s gyrating Elvis, complete with gold jacket, or a '70s karate Elvis, complete with jumpsuit. These pastor Elvis imitators used as many song titles and cliché Elvis sayings as possible in the ceremony before they sang songs to the couple such as "Teddy Bear."

Elvis has become an inseparable part of the Las Vegas culture. His image is everywhere and impersonators are found in the acts and on the streets trying to lure people into businesses. But probably the best tribute to the King is the Cirque du Soleil tribute show. While his first effort in Las Vegas may have been less than stellar, the lasting impression Elvis left has never been equaled. In fact, in Las Vegas it can truly be said that Elvis has never left the building.

A SEARCH FOR SHOWGIRLS

1957

Anticipation mixed excitement with thick cigar smoke, filling the small room. The walls were covered in red felt wallpaper and heavy red curtains ran from floor to ceiling on either side of the stage. Men dressed in cowboy hats and suits puffed thick cigars and escorted women clothed in long, flowing gowns and high heels. Maitre d's adorned in black tuxedos and bowties showed guests to seats in the crowded showroom, sliding their palms across those of the guests, in a secret exchange of currency meant to procure prime seating.

Women dressed in short black skirts roamed the room with trays resting on their hips and strapped to their necks. They offered cigarettes, cigars, and matches. Others, dressed in revealing shirts, took drink orders and delivered cocktails. As the curtains opened, the room turned its attention to the stage, ready for a night of exciting entertainment. And that is just what they got. Women emerged from the curtains sliding gracefully on stage, adorned with shiny headdresses, elaborate jeweled gowns, and long sleek gloves. And as Frank Sinatra entered the stage and began to sing, the crowd exploded in applause. Opening night of the Sands Texas Copa Girls was a resounding success.

The excitement of that evening began long before the curtains rose. It was, in fact, the brainchild of a Texas gambler and a New York nightclub boss. While Jake Freeman had made his money in Texas oil, gambling brought him further west to Las Vegas where in 1951 he purchased a plot of land for $15,000. His intent was to build a world-class resort, and he spent $600,000 to turn that land into the Sands Hotel and Casino. His partner and co-owner, Jack Entratter, was an imposing figure, more than six feet tall with a deep, baritone voice. Before moving to Las Vegas, Entratter had been general manager of the famous Copacabana club in New York City.

The two made the Sands a rousing success from the moment of its opening on December 12, 1952. When it opened, the Sands was considered the most luxurious resort on the Strip, if not the world. It had copper light fixtures and an Italian marble entrance. Entratter had managed to bring the entertainers he booked in New York to play in the Sands's showroom, called the Copa Room, loosely named after the New York club.

But Freeman knew that oil was king and he wanted that Texas money in his casino. In 1957 Freeman and Entratter took out advertisements in newspapers in Dallas, Fort Worth, Houston, and El Paso, inviting Texas money to come to the Sands to see the Texas Copa Girls. "This man knew what he was doing," recalled Virginia James, a Sands Texas Copa Girl, speaking of Freeman. "He knew that if their girl was appearing at the Sands, they were going to bring their money and come see their girl. And they did. I mean, it was a good idea."

Freeman and Entratter knew that they had to get original Texas girls for their new show or it would not attract the intended crowd. The two men also knew that getting the girls to come to Las Vegas would be easy, but finding them would be another matter altogether. But the resourceful Entratter had an idea. He proposed a contest, much like a beauty contest, that would attract the women they were looking for. Freeman agreed and Entratter took out advertisements on radio stations in the same major Texas cities in which they had placed the newspaper ads. The radio ads were directed to young women. It invited women to "come and be a dancer at the Sands, meet all the stars." He also placed advertisements in the local papers, complete with an application to be filled out and mailed back to the Sands.

The contest worked. Freeman and Entratter received thousands of applications. They picked through the stack and chose the girls they liked best. Those girls were sent a letter from the Sands telling them that they would be competing for the final cut. The letter also informed them that they were expected to dress in either a bathing suit or shorts and a shirt. They were also told to bring a dress. "They wanted to see you in high heels and hose," recalled Virginia James.

Entratter decided to choose each girl personally. His plan was to go to each radio station in each city and choose one girl from that contest. He started the search in El Paso, Texas. The contest was held at KTSM radio station. While Entratter's plan may have been sound on paper, it was much harder to implement. Almost immediately in El Paso he ran into trouble deciding between three girls. As the girls paraded in front of him in their chosen bathing suits and dresses, Entratter, much to his surprise was unable to narrow the field. The girls looked very different in person and Entratter just couldn't pick. The girls were nervous. They knew that only one of them would be chosen and Entratter's indecision took the stress to a much higher level.

After looking at the girls over and over again, he managed to narrow the field down to two, Virginia and another girl named Mara.

Finally, after much internal debate, Entratter made his decision saying, "Virginia, I have to have you. But, Mara, you are so pretty, I'm going to take you, too." The girls were ecstatic. Entratter had the same trouble deciding on girls in both Dallas and Houston. He picked a set of twins in each city. Before he returned to Las Vegas, Entratter had one more change. Back then Virginia's last name was Moody. Entratter took one look at her and said "you look like a Virginia James" and the name stuck.

Virginia and the other girls went back to their daily lives and jobs awaiting a phone call from the Sands. Because the contest had been such a big deal, the girls became celebrities in their hometowns. "Boy, were we big shots at home," recalled Virginia. When the call finally came, Virginia and the other girls were flown to Las Vegas to begin training. The change was dramatic for the young woman. "When we flew in, McCarran Airport wasn't here. It was called McCarran Airport, but it was a little house, a little shack," recalled Virginia. "And there was nothing, just dirt. No grass around it, no nothing; just a little tiny shack."

The girls were picked up in a limo and taken immediately to the Bali Hai hotel. They were booked rooms and told not to go into any hotels, especially the Sands. "We weren't to go to any of the hotels because they didn't want anybody to see us because it was going to be a big thing, and they had invited every big Texas man," recalled Virginia. But the limo driver did take the girls past the Sands so that they could see their name on the billboard at the front of the hotel. They couldn't contain their excitement as they saw the "Sands Texas Copa Girls" as big as life on the marquee.

The showgirls and dancers weren't given much time to dwell in the excitement of their new surroundings. The girls were escorted by limo to a dance studio where they were told they would be opening with Frank Sinatra in two weeks. They were thrust into a grueling schedule of rehearsals and dancing schools. The Sands was noted for its stars, and these girls would be dancing with those stars, major stars, and they were expected to be perfect right away. The problem was, few if any of them had any real experience.

Bobby Gilbert and Rene Stewart worked as choreographers for the show. "They had a dancing school here," recalled Virginia. "They knew that they had a bunch of greenhorns, green Texas horns, but they were patient. They took us to the dance class and had us take classes with other people, just to do little bits of everything to get the feel. I mean, none of us had ever been on stage."

The girls were broken into two groups—dancers and showgirls—and asked to perform many different tasks. The distinction was based on what they did on stage. Showgirls paraded in elaborate costumes and dancers actually danced. The two groups typically took turns on stage, with showgirls strolling in the background while performers, like Frank Sinatra, sang ballads. Dancers also performed with stars, but those numbers were typically upbeat. Dancers also performed while stars took breaks.

When the girls finally went on stage it was exciting. "The curtain went up, and we were standing in back of the curtain. I thought my heart would drop. Really I did," recalled Virginia. "And then the music was on and everybody started dancing. And you just started smiling and just really got with it."

One of the most difficult costumes worn by the Copa Showgirls was a sleek white satin, almost wedding-like, dress attached to a large hoop laced in red velvet. The dress was form fitting down to the upper thigh where it suddenly turned into the hoop. The dress itself was part of the hoop, and it forced the showgirls to walk gracefully while encased in shining fabric.

Unlike their modern counterparts, the Sands Texas Copa Girls did not perform topless. In fact, there was no nudity of any kind on any Las Vegas stage in the 1950s. Dancers wore costumes that covered them as much as possible while still allowing freedom of movement. Showgirls were fully clothed with hats, gloves, and stockings. The only parts of the body that were exposed were the neck, head, and shoulders. "Even the makeup was different," recalled dancer Denise Clair Garon. "We were so close to the audience. The lights were not as bright as they are now. The heavy, thick, bizarre eye makeup was not necessary."

The girls were paid about $150 a week and treated like stars. Their expected duties did not end with their performance on stage however. They also had a social function called mixing. "In the intermission between the first and second show, the girls would sit in the lounges where there were other acts performing . . . just to decorate the hotel," recalled Carmon Messwab, a musician of the time. When the show let out, the Sands Texas Copa Girls were also expected to change into formal gowns and mingle with the high-rolling guests on the floor of the casino in the table game area. "About an hour to an hour and a half after the second show they were expected to stay on the premises," recalled Messwab.

In 1958 Freeman died and Entratter took over the casino as president, with Carl Cohen, the casino boss, as the vice president. The Sands continued its success and expansion with the Copa Room becoming famous as the home of the Rat Pack. The Texas Copa Girls disbanded, but the Copa Girls themselves continued to thrive, performing on stage nightly. In 1967 billionaire Howard Hughes bought the Sands for $23 million. Although he died before he could see it, Freeman's $15,000 investment was a gamble that paid off.

THE SUMMIT

1960

Five men gathered on stage at the Sands Copa Room in Las Vegas. They were dressed in black tuxedo jackets with shiny lapels, their white shirts decorated with black bowties. They stood next to each other sharing two microphones. Instead of doing any type of rehearsed act, the men taunt and tease each other, telling stories to the delight of the crowd. They create a party atmosphere in which they are the hosts. For an hour and a half each evening, two times a night, they invite the audience into their lives, these five playboys. It is a carefree life that every member of the audience envies, a life where the Rat Pack rules.

In 1960s Las Vegas showcased the most famous talent in the world and the Sands Hotel and Casino was the hippest place to be. Five stars were filming a movie called *Ocean's Eleven* in Las Vegas: Frank Sinatra, Dean Martin, Sammy Davis Jr., Peter Lawford, and Joey Bishop. In the film twelve war buddies led by Danny Ocean, played by Frank Sinatra, plot to rob five of the biggest casinos in Las Vegas, all at the same time.

The movie had an ensemble cast, including Angie Dickinson and Cesar Romero, and was filmed almost entirely in the Las Vegas casinos featured in the movie. Being true entertainers, and taking advantage of the situation, the men filmed mostly in the day and entertained in the casinos at night. The group began hanging out together more and more frequently, backstage at each other's shows. They became known for their antics, which included all night parties, drinking, and womanizing.

Sinatra, being the oldest and arguably the most famous at the time, was crowned the leader. The group often referred to themselves as the "clan," but the press started to call them the "Rat Pack," reportedly because Judy Garland told them they looked like a pack of rats after seeing them emerge from an all night party. It was a name that stuck. Among themselves, however, the group would refer to their meetings as "the summit," the name coined by Sinatra, who didn't like the racial implications associated with the word "clan." Because Sinatra called the group "the summit," they started to call him the "Chairman of the Board."

One evening during an especially long summit meeting, the chairman had an idea. He proposed that the five should appear on stage at his regular haunt, the Copa Room. The men agreed and Sinatra arranged the event. On the first night the Copa Room presented the Rat Pack, it was filled to capacity. Guests and celebrities alike had gathered to see the group perform. Nervous energy abounded as the excitement of seeing their favorite performers grew. When the boys walked on stage, drinks and cigarettes in hand, they were met with cheers and applause.

The secret to the Rat Pack's success was not their entertainment ability. Two of them (Sinatra and Martin) were great singers and one (Davis) was a phenomenal singer and dancer, but the remaining two had no real singing or dancing ability whatsoever. What made the group so famous was their ability to create a mystique—one that every member of the audience wanted to be involved with.

As is the case with most entertainers, the Rat Pack went to bed when most people were getting ready for work. But these boys made it sound like they were doing it by choice, not because it was the schedule that best fit into the lifestyle of the typical entertainer. They also managed to blur the lines between work and play. In fact Sammy Davis Jr. would often say on stage, "Ladies and gentlemen what happens here on stage happens off stage."

What made the members of the Rat Pack special was that they were respectable although somewhat irreverent rebels. Davis routinely told the audience that he represented the NAACP. Frank commonly called Davis "Smokey" and once said, as the spotlight was closing in on Davis, "Keep smiling Smokey so everybody knows where you are." This was followed by, "Why don't you be yourself and eat some ribs." Sinatra's comments commonly caused Davis to laugh hysterically. In one show Davis began a song. As the music started, Davis sang "I'm not much to look at," to which Martin immediately commented "You're goddamned right." This sent the audience into a roar. Davis attempted to finish the song, but Martin and Sinatra kept up constant interruption, so he finally gave up. Davis turned his back to the audience and said to the bandleader "We might as well do the other song; they won't let me finish this one." To which Martin again responded "You're goddamned right." Another time Sinatra told Davis to "hurry up Sam the watermelon's getting warm." Davis responded "Well it's better than eating pizza every night." To which Sinatra countered "Yeah but we don't have to spit out the crust." The crowd laughed and Davis shot a twisted face to Sinatra.

The Rat Pack dressed in fancy suits, drank expensive liquor, smoked the best cigarettes and cigars, and got the classiest women. They were the James Bonds of their time. They also transformed Las Vegas, bringing it into the era of glitz and glamour.

Las Vegas was invented in the 1940s when the El Rancho and The Last Frontier evolved the saloons on Fremont Street into resorts, creating the famous Las Vegas Strip. At the time Las Vegas was a true western town and these two resorts embraced that western theme. In 1945 the Flamingo moved away from the western theme and opened the door for Las Vegas to become a resort destination.

The 1950s brought one of Las Vegas's first booms and an influx of casinos onto the scene. The downtown area saw the opening of Binion's Horseshoe and the Fremont, while the Strip saw the opening of the Stardust, the Sands, the Hacienda, the Dunes, the Tropicana, the Sahara, and the Riviera. With the casinos came the stars who performed for large paychecks in the showrooms. "The money was enormous," recalled comedian Red Buttons. "Four weeks in Vegas could buy you a Third World country."

The late 1950s and early 60s also brought the age of adult entertainment, as casinos started offering topless showgirls. It also, strangely enough, brought in class as guests wore evening gowns and jackets to the shows and even in the casinos. In this atmosphere Frank and his pals were a perfect fit. More and more celebrities came to town to see them perform, and being there so often, those celebrities started falling in love with Las Vegas.

But celebrities weren't the only ones interested in the Rat Pack. A young Democratic candidate for president by the name of John F. Kennedy came to Las Vegas to campaign. While there, he decided to stop in at the Sands to see his brother-in-law perform with the rest of the Rat Pack. Six years earlier Kennedy's younger sister had married the British-born Peter Lawford. Kennedy watched the show and when it was over joined the boys for an informal party. In turn the Rat Pack did rallies and helped campaign for Kennedy. The Rat Pack even sang the National Anthem to open the Democratic Convention in 1960.

After his election, Kennedy returned to Las Vegas every so often. One such occasion was remembered fondly by Sammy Davis Jr. Because the Copa Room was so small, the entire Rat Pack shared one single dressing room. While they were preparing for the show, Sinatra came in and told them that JFK was in attendance. At a certain point in the show all the celebrities in the audience were introduced by the members of the Rat Pack in a round-robin style. Everyone naturally assumed that Sinatra would introduce the president. Instead he walked to the bar that was set up on stage and poured himself a drink. Martin and Davis looked at each other, wondering what their leader was doing. Without looking up Sinatra passed the honor to Davis. "Smokey, you introduce the president."

Before the end of the '60s, the Rat Pack's time had come to an end. In 1967 the Sands cut off Sinatra's line of credit. Frank responded in true Sinatra style by throwing furniture at pit boss Carl Cohen. Sinatra left the Sands and signed a contract with the year-old Caesars Palace. The rest of the Rat Pack did not follow. Although the days of the Rat Pack were over, the boys had made their impact on the town and forever changed the look of Las Vegas. While Vegas eventually moved on, reinventing itself many times over, many visitors and locals alike still long for the days when Frank, Dean, Sammy, Joey, and Peter reigned supreme. Shows imitating the Rat Pack still perform in casino lounges.

A MYSTERIOUS BILLIONAIRE
REFUSES TO LEAVE

1966

In November 1966, two of the most important men in Las Vegas met to solve the biggest problem they had ever faced. While most of their counterparts struggled to fill their hotel rooms during the notoriously slow pre-holiday season, Moe Dalitz and Ruby Kolod, owners of one of the most luxurious hotel casinos in Las Vegas, had the exact opposite problem. They had a guest in the top two floors of their hotel who refused to leave. While most people would be thrilled to have that problem, the owners of the Desert Inn knew that the longer their guest stayed the more money they lost. They needed that man to leave and they needed him to leave right away. The only problem was the man occupying those entire two floors was no ordinary person. He was quite possibly the richest man in America.

When the sixty-one-year-old Howard Hughes arrived at the Desert Inn that Thanksgiving weekend, his original plan was to stay about ten days and to look around for investment opportunities. It was a cold winter day when the train pulled into the station at

4:00 a.m. The time had been picked on purpose to ensure that no unwanted gawkers lurked around the station. His unusually short train consisted of two private luxury cars and a locomotive engine.

Hughes was used to stepping triumphantly, after having broken world records, from the cockpits of planes he designed and flew. He had also acquired quite a reputation as a playboy in the 1940s and '50s. But it was a different Howard Hughes who arrived at the North Las Vegas train station. Sometime in the early 1960s Hughes had become a recluse, hardly being seen in public. He was completely terrified of germs and was addicted to painkillers. On that cold November morning Howard Hughes didn't step from the train like a would-be conqueror. The thin, pale man was carried on a stretcher, trembling from the cold desert air, to a waiting van that took him to a Las Vegas luxury resort. While he may not have looked like a conqueror at the time, his actions soon proved otherwise.

Dalitz and Kolod didn't care what shape their guest was in. All they knew was the busy Christmas and New Year seasons were quickly approaching and Hughes occupied the rooms that would normally be rented to high rollers. Gamblers, who unlike Hughes and his staff of mainly LDS members (Mormons), would spend hundreds of thousands of dollars in the casino. Dalitz and Kolod were furious. "We had already confirmed many reservations for those two floors," recalled Dalitz, "in anticipation of Mr. Hughes moving on."

The two men tried to wait Hughes out, but after several weeks he and his staff showed no sign of leaving and the owners had all that they could take. They marched through the ochre-colored halls lit with fine glass fixtures, taking the private elevator to the top floor and Hughes's suite. But when they approached Hughes's rooms, they were not allowed to enter. Hughes refused to give the two owners any clear date when he and his staff would vacate the rooms. With their patience at an end, Dalitz and Kolod demanded that Hughes leave: "Get the hell out or we'll throw your butt out," Kolod told Hughes.

Hughes was undaunted. In 1966 Howard Hughes was one of the richest men in America. He had just received a settlement check of over $540 million for the sale of his controlling shares of Trans World Airlines, better known as TWA. The check delivered to Hughes was the largest ever made out to an individual, but all it meant to Hughes was that he would have to pay millions of dollars in federal and state taxes if he didn't invest the money quickly.

Howard Hughes was no stranger to Las Vegas, having spent much time there in the 1940s and '50s. While he spent time at the gaming tables, he was for the most part an unlucky gambler who didn't take well to losing and was known to be very vocal when he lost. Although he did gamble, he was most often seen in the company of a beautiful woman at a show or in a restaurant. Hughes lived in California, but wasn't happy with his status there. He complained that he was tired of being "a small fish in the big pond of Southern California." Hughes had a goal. He wanted people to pay attention when he spoke and he saw an opportunity to make that happen in Las Vegas.

When Dalitz and Kolod left, Hughes contacted Robert Maheu, a former FBI agent and his chief of security. He was furious with the owners and yelled at Maheu. "It's your problem. You work it out." Maheu knew that he needed some clout to handle "his" problem, so he contacted Teamsters president Jimmy Hoffa. Moe Dalitz was rumored to have connections in organized crime, as was Hoffa whose Teamsters funded the building of many Las Vegas properties. Hoffa made a phone call to Dalitz and asked him to leave his friends alone. While Hoffa was able to buy Maheu and Hughes some time, the inevitable soon happened.

Early into the new year of 1967, Dalitz and Kolod again called for Hughes's departure and nothing even Hoffa could say would change that. Maheu finally contacted Hughes and told him, "If you want a place to sleep, you'd damn well better buy the hotel." After months of negotiating Hughes did just that; he bought the Desert Inn from Dalitz for more than $13 million, most of that in cash. What followed was an almost complete transformation of Las Vegas.

In the 1960s organized crime had a strong hold in the casino industry. Money was being skimmed from profits at an alarming rate. While millions of dollars were being made, the State of Nevada and the State Gaming Commission were seeing little to none of it. However, with Howard Hughes, they, along with Governor Paul Laxalt, saw an opportunity to change that. Hughes presented them with the ability to rid their town of organized crime. They would be able to make sure that casino owners were "so clean they squeaked."

Initially the Nevada Gaming Control Board was offended when Hughes ignored their requirement to appear in public to apply for a gaming license. However, when Governor Laxalt pleaded on Hughes's behalf, the board eventually relented. To allow Hughes to have a gaming license, they disregarded every rule they had put in place to prevent mobster ownership of a casino. They certified Hughes without making him pass any of their tests and background checks.

Hughes made Maheu head of his Nevada operations. Delighted at the tax advantages he gained from the purchase of the Desert Inn, Hughes asked Maheu "How many more of these toys are available?" Maheu knew that Hughes hated paying taxes and would be willing to invest in anything that would save him from paying them. "Hughes would use every gimmick in the book; he'd pay someone half a million dollars if they could help him avoid paying $10 worth of taxes."

The Mafia tried to influence Hughes, but Maheu, being former FBI, was not intimidated. When Johnny Rosselli, a known Mafia front person, tried to tell Maheu who would be the new casino manager at the Desert Inn, Maheu told him to go to hell. The next three purchases by Hughes proved instrumental in the change of Las Vegas. He bought three properties reputedly run by organized crime: the Sands Hotel and Casino for $14.6 million (including 183 acres of prime real estate behind the property—which eventually became the Howard Hughes Center), the Castaways for $3 million, and the Frontier for $14 million.

While many believed that Hughes chose properties to buy based on advice from his close confidantes, Maheu had another idea. "If you look at what we bought, you'll find that we must have known something." Maheu suggested that Hughes followed a blueprint to get rid of organized crime in Las Vegas, based on a study commissioned by attorney general Robert Kennedy. The study claimed that the best way to clean up Las Vegas was to buy the Mob out, and as Maheu stated, "who is better equipped with the money than Hughes?"

Whether Maheu was correct or not, Hughes's next purchase was done more for convenience than because of secret plans to rid the town of an unsavory element. Hughes kept his operation set up in the top floors of the Desert Inn, which was directly across the street from the Silver Slipper. The Silver Slipper had a very notable marquee that was topped by a huge rotating Cinderella-like slipper, adorned by thousands of bright lights. Hughes hated the marquee. The shadows created by the rotating shoe hit his window and disturbed his slumber. He sent Maheu a telegram. "I want you to buy that place, that damn sign is driving me crazy, it goes round and round and round." Hughes paid more than $5 million for a good night's sleep.

Hughes bought only one more casino, the Landmark, but it was not all he bought in Las Vegas. During his stay he purchased an airline, an airport, gold and silver mines, a motel, a restaurant, and a local television station. He also bought thousands of acres of land in the area adjacent to the Red Rocks Recreation Area that his corporation eventually developed into a master planned community called Summerland after his death. The purchase of so many casinos in such a short time spelled the death of organized crime in Las Vegas and opened the door for a corporate takeover. Pleased with Hughes's results, the Nevada Legislature passed the Corporate Gaming Act, which allowed corporations to bypass the financial background checks previously required to own a casino.

Hughes left Las Vegas the same way he came, shrouded in mystery. Almost four years to the date that he arrived, Hughes, a shadow of the man that first came to Las Vegas in the 1940s, was placed on a stretcher and transported in a van to Nellis Air Force Base where a private jet waited. Hughes never returned to Las Vegas.

AN EVEL JUMP

1967

On a bright sunny day in December, a motorcycle rolled slowly to the top of a ramp until its front tire rested at the edge. Its rider was dressed in a white, one-piece jumpsuit, with stripes running down the sides. The man, who was standing slightly as he climbed the ramp, sat back down on the bike and looked over the scene in front of him. Fountains, shooting flowing water into the air, decorated an expanding pool. The fountains adorned the entrance to Caesars Palace, one of the most elaborate casinos in Las Vegas.

The man looked over the crowd of onlookers who had gathered to watch the event. He took a deep breath and released the brake. The bike rolled back down the ramp. When he reached the bottom, he turned and rode back to the designated starting point. He bowed his head, said a quiet prayer, took another deep breath, and hit the gas.

Many conversations in Las Vegas tend to involve the words "you're crazy." Such was the case when the man known as Evel Knievel first approached Joe Sarno, owner and CEO of Caesars Palace. Sarno was a gambler who had made a small fortune with a chain of cabana motor inns. He was a flamboyant man known for big ideas and living life to the fullest. Las Vegas in the 1950s had a noticeable western theme. While the casinos had taken a step away from the saloons, Sarno saw that step as far too small. "Las Vegas had done the wild western motif to death. What it needed was a little true opulence." And a little true opulence was what Las Vegas got.

Sarno envisioned a resort where people lived the life of the Roman Empire. "We wanted to create the feeling that everyone in the hotel was a Caesar," recalled Sarno. So he named the resort Caesars Palace, leaving the apostrophe off intentionally. Alan Feldman, senior vice president of MGM Mirage, credited Sarno with being the first to recognize the real draw to Las Vegas. "It wasn't the gambling that attracted people. It was the fantasy. [Sarno] knew that if the majority of people in the world could live like Caesar, they would live like Caesar." On August 5, 1966, Sarno opened Caesars Palace. It was the first of the themed casinos that eventually became synonymous with Las Vegas. Sarno managed to re-create the opulent life of Rome. The buildings were adorned with statues, including one of Caesar himself inviting people into the resort.

But at Caesars Palace it was the many fountains at the front entrance to the casino that stood out the most. There were eighteen fountains in total, but the main body of fountains that first greeted guests from Las Vegas Boulevard drew the most attention. A large pool of water housed seven fountains. Four large circular fountains shot individual streams of water ten feet in the air, the water falling in an arc toward their center. Three even larger fountains stood between the circular fountains, shooting large geysers of water more than thirty feet, straight up.

Knievel first got the idea to jump the fountains while visiting Las Vegas in November 1967 to watch a boxing match. After the fight, Knievel and a group of friends went to Caesars Palace where he saw the fountains and launched the idea to jump them. But Knievel had yet to reach the fame he would eventually achieve and he knew that getting permission to jump those fountains would not be easy.

Evel Knievel was born Robert Craig Knievel in Butte, Montana. He was a natural athlete who competed in track in both high school and the military. In the late 1950s Knievel tried his hand at professional hockey with the Charlotte Clippers. His tenure with the team was short lived and he eventually returned to Butte to form a semi-professional team called the Butte Bombers. Even at an early age Knievel showed a propensity for being a daredevil. In 1959 he entered, and won, the Northern Rocky Mountain Ski Association ski jumping competition. But Knievel had a difficult time finding his true calling, and like many wanderers he eventually found his way into a life of crime.

"I robbed so many safes in Oregon that one of the newspapers said it looked like somebody was dropping bombs through the roofs," Knievel stated in an interview with *Esquire* magazine. Reports of FBI investigations plagued Knievel for most of his life. He told *Sports Illustrated* that while he got away with it, "it's not the right way of life." It was in those years that Knievel earned his moniker of "Evel."

In 1965 Knievel opened a Honda motorcycle shop. It was the turn that eventually led him down the road to fame. He became fascinated with motorcycles and formed a group called Evel Knievel's Motorcycle Daredevils, which was based on Joey Chitwood's Automotive Show, which he had seen in his youth. In an interview with the *New Yorker*, Knievel explained the shows the daredevils put on. "We had a traveling show. I'd do five or six stunts—ride through fire walls, jump over boxes of live rattlesnakes and land between two chained mountain lions, get towed down a drag strip at 200 mph."

The jumps got bigger and the bikes stronger. During his days with the daredevils, Knievel devised a plan to build a winged jetbike and jump it over the Grand Canyon. He wrote to Secretary of the Interior Stuart Udall for permission. It wasn't granted. "He did not share my enthusiasm," recalled Knievel.

Assuming that he would get the same response from Joe Sarno, Knievel figured that he needed to appear more legit, so he created a dummy corporation called Evel Knievel Enterprises. He also invented the name of a law firm that he used to place the phone call to Sarno. When Knievel's fictitious attorney made the initial call, Sarno was about as enthusiastic as Udall. Knievel wasn't finished however. He placed additional calls claiming to represent both *Sports Illustrated* and the American Broadcasting Company inquiring about the jump.

Sarno eventually agreed to meet with Knievel, and when he did he found a kindred spirit. The two men hit it off and a deal was struck for Knievel to jump the fountains at Caesars Palace. The jump took place on December 31, 1967. Excited about the agreement, Knievel figured that ABC would jump at the chance to feature the event on their *Wide World of Sports*. They didn't. Knievel was a relentless salesman however, and he managed to convince ABC executives to review the film if Knievel filmed the event.

Knievel got his friend director John Derek to film the event on a budget. In fact, according to legend, Derek's wife Linda Evans, of *Dynasty* fame, was the person who actually filmed the now famous footage. While this is most likely not true, it does add to the Vegas mystique. Knievel also notified the local press and with the help of Sarno publicized the jump through the casino. They also picked a perfect time to do the jump as Las Vegas was crowded over the busy New Year's Eve weekend.

The ramps were placed toward the middle of the fountains so that Knievel could jump over the lower fountains without being hit by the water shooting from the higher fountains. The distance between the two ramps was more than 140 feet. It was the largest distance Knievel had jumped to date. When the ramps were built Knievel smiled. He knew that if he made the jump he would be famous.

A showman, Knievel put on quite a spectacle. He greeted the large crowd with a showgirl on each arm at his pre-jump show. When the show was over, he took his motorcycle to the starting point of the jump and positioned it toward the ramp. As he sat at the starting point Knievel recited the prayer he used at every jump, "God take care of me. Here I come." Knievel revved the throttle on the bike and let go of the brake.

Knievel's approach was flawless. As the bike left the ramp he lifted the front end and stood slightly, shifting his weight to the front of the bike to help gain the needed distance. He cleared the fountains easily, as cameras clicked, creating some of the most spectacular photos in the history of his profession. As Knievel approached the ramp his tire was still flying high. Looking at the jump from the landing ramp, onlookers could see the Sands and Flamingo casinos clearly in the background. It looked to all present that the spectacular jump was going to be picture perfect. Unfortunately, that was not the case.

The cause of the failed jump would be debated for many years to come. Some said the back tire slid on impact, others claimed that Knievel overshot the ramp and that his front tire was too high, causing it to slam down when the bike contacted the ramp. What is known for sure is that when the bike came down on the ramp, Knievel was still in a slight standing posture. The impact caused him to slam into the seat of the bike. The front of the bike pulled away from him and Knievel was almost immediately forced to let go of the handlebars. The force shot him head first over the handlebars toward the right side of the bike, his arms stretched out front.

Momentum forced his legs high into the air as the front wheel of the bike turned violently right then left and then straightened out.

Knievel came down hard on his shoulders as the chin guard of his helmet slammed into his chest. The rest of his body crashed hard on the asphalt and he tumbled violently while his bike rolled forward. Knievel continued to tumble until finally coming to a stop. Remarkably, the bike never hit or ran over Knievel. In fact, it continued on a straight line, until at one point the front wheel wobbled, the bike leaned left, flipped over to the right, and fell. The bike continued to skid and even flipped over one more time before it came to a stop.

Rescue workers rushed in and doused the bike with fire extinguishers. Knievel was immediately rushed to the hospital. He had fractured his pelvis and one of the bones in his leg. Additionally he broke a wrist and both ankles and also suffered a concussion that placed him in a twenty-nine-day coma. Ironically Knievel became more famous for the wreck than he might have for the jump had he been successful. ABC eventually bought the rights and Knievel's career was launched.

Knievel never repeated the jump. He died in 2007. He also never jumped the Grand Canyon as he had hoped. Both feats were left to his son, Robbie Knievel, who took up the family business and successfully completed both jumps.

A CASINO CATCHES FIRE

1980

Guests awoke to a new day of rest and relaxation in the twenty-six-story, two-million-square-foot MGM Grand Hotel Casino. It was a crisp 38-degree Las Vegas morning. Employees walked to the hotel from their designated parking and added to the more than five thousand people who were already inside the hotel and casino. Restaurants geared up for breakfast. Guests stood in line and waited to be seated. The Orleans Coffee Shop was open and had already seated fifty guests. The Deli, located next to the coffee shop, was one of the few restaurants that had not yet opened. In the Deli two friction-damaged wires caused a spark. The spark grew quickly into flames. As guests were served their coffee and eggs, a disaster was underway that would cause the second largest loss of life in a hotel fire in U.S. history.

The problem had started much earlier than that day in November. Vibration from a machine that powered a refrigerated display case had caused wires to rub together. The display case was in the Deli and the wires, located in the wall, went unnoticed. As the wires worked against each other, they eventually wore so much that on November 21, 1980, they caused an arc that started a fire. In what seems strange by modern-day standards, building codes in the 1970s, when the MGM was built, did not require sprinkler systems or readily available fire extinguishers. Unencumbered by water, the fire found a ready supply of fuel in the plastic, paper, and wood building materials.

Employees noticed the fire around 7:00 a.m., and by the time the Clark County Fire Department arrived at 7:17 a.m., thick black smoke was already bellowing from the building. As Captain Rex Smith and his crew entered the casino, they were faced with a fireball rolling toward them from the Deli. An evacuation was immediately ordered. It took Captain Smith and his crew twenty-five seconds to exit the casino and reach the fire trucks. They were closely followed by the fireball shooting out the front of the building, destroying everything in its path. The ball of fire had traveled a distance of 336 feet in only twenty-five seconds.

When told a fire had started, MGM employee Chef Oborn grabbed a nearby wall-mounted fire hose and rushed toward the flames. Luckily, he was stopped by a fellow employee who warned him not to fight an electrical fire with water. Given a constant supply of fuel and little resistance, the fire spread quickly, often at a rate of fifteen feet per second, and easily reached temperatures of over 2,000 degrees.

Instead of rushing out themselves, the employees put the safety of the guests ahead of their own and immediately pitched in to help the guests reach the exits. As the fire spread, several employees were astonished that so many guests were unwilling to leave their slot machines or the plastic chips representing the money they had won. One guest would not leave until the pit boss personally vouched for the amount of chips he had in front of him. Another continued to pull the handle of a slot machine even though the guest was warned by an employee that "people were dying over there." As employees helped guests to evacuate, security struggled to gain control of the situation. Looters rushed in to grab what they could get—money from the gaming tables, jewelry from the guest rooms—some did not make it back outside.

The very thing that allows Las Vegas to be an entertainment mecca in the scorching desert was the cause of the MGM Grand's demise. The air conditioning return ducts funneled the deadly smoke from the casino into many of the rooms in the north wing of the hotel. In some cases, the smoke was filtered, but even then toxic carbon monoxide was pumped into the rooms. Guests who ran from their rooms to the stairwells quickly found them engulfed in smoke. Some guests headed for the stairwells only to have the exit doors slam and lock shut behind them. Once inside, screaming guests found themselves surrounded by a thick cloud of black smoke. Their only choice was to climb higher and try to outrun the rising cloud. Many became quickly disoriented. Trapped with no escape, they died in the stairwells.

As the heavy black smoke passed through the ventilation system and seeped under the guest room doors, many took their chances out the windows. They leaped to their deaths rather than face an inevitable suffocation. Some guests simply died in their sleep unaware of the black death that rolled into their rooms.

An unidentified construction worker was doing work on a scaffold outside the hotel where an expansion project was underway. As the black smoke bellowed from the rooms below him, the worker reacted quickly, putting the lives of the guests ahead of his own. He pulled guests from their windows onto his scaffold. When the guests were safe, the worker told them "You're okay, don't panic. I've got to get the babies first." The panicking guests watched in amazement as the worker climbed back into the hotel from the scaffold. He told the guests "I'll be back for you." When he returned, he had three boys, one six-years-old, one twelve-years-old, and one four-months-old.

As the smoke poured into the rooms, many guests had few choices left in their struggle to stay alive. They threw televisions and furniture through the windows to create ventilation. Shattered glass filled the air as the construction worker lowered his rescues from the scaffold to thê ground below. He covered the children with pillows and blankets he had pulled from the room to protect them from the falling shards of glass. A witness overheard the worker as he attempted to calm the children. "This is a good adventure for you."

Television cameras responded immediately and broadcast the disaster nationally. Las Vegas residents saw the fire on television and immediately got involved. The owner of a local helicopter business rallied his pilots to the scene. Guests pleaded for the pilots to rescue them from the floors of the hotel, but the blades of the helicopters prevented the pilots from getting that close. Instead, the pilots took their helicopters to the roof. They rescued guests and employees stranded for more than two hours in the upper levels of the hotel. Helicopters were also provided by the Las Vegas Metropolitan Police Department, Nellis Air Force Base, and services as far away as San Diego, California.

Two refrigerated semi trailers were donated by a local trucking company and were turned into a makeshift morgue. Three deputy coroners were sent to the scene of the fire to identify bodies. Eighty-five people died as a result of the fire or fire-related injuries. Seventy-nine of those deaths were a result of smoke or carbon monoxide inhalation. More than seven hundred guests and employees were injured. Three hundred firefighters reported symptoms of smoke inhalation and fourteen were hospitalized.

In the end, the twenty-four floors of the hotel were untouched by the fire, damaged instead by the thick black smoke that filled the return air ducts. The north end of the casino was destroyed. All that remained was a black swamp created when the thousands of gallons of water that was dumped on the fire mixed with ash. Strangely enough, the south side of the casino came through relatively unscathed. And in true Las Vegas fashion, a day after the fire, MGM Grand vice president Steve Booke proclaimed that the showroom showed little damage and could easily house a show that night. Most of the restaurants on the south end experienced little damage as well.

While it was the air conditioning and lack of sprinklers that helped the fire spread, it was the mild Las Vegas weather that prevented an even greater disaster. The lack of wind stopped ventilation from spreading the smoke faster and to a greater area. As a result of the fire at the MGM Grand, building codes throughout the United States were updated to mandate sprinklers, fire extinguishers, and emergency warning systems. While devastating, the fire helped Las Vegas to become a city that uses the most advanced fire protection systems available.

THE CASINO INDUSTRY
GETS A MAKEOVER

1988

A silver Mercedes turned off the Las Vegas Strip onto the grounds of the Sands Hotel and Casino. It came to a stop only a few feet onto the property, directly under the casino's flashing marquee. The driver exited the car, carefully closed the front door behind him, and sat on the hood. He folded his arms across his chest and stared at the 102-acre lot across the street that he had just purchased from the Hughes Corporation—formerly owned by Howard Hughes. The property was mostly bare except for a small and very old casino called the Castaways.

The words "I look for the conflict" popped into his head. They were a response to a question posed by Johnny Carson to Neil Simon about how he writes comedy. The man slowly surveyed the landscape and allowed his mind to search for something new, something different, something that would make people want to walk inside his new hotel casino. From out of nowhere a song bounced into his head, "Bali Hai" from the musical *South Pacific*. It proved to be the inspiration for one of the greatest makeovers in Las Vegas history.

The Las Vegas of the early 1980s was a place full of neon and flashing white lights. Many of the casinos still embodied the spa resort style found in Palm Springs and Scottsdale. Few properties had guest room towers; instead bungalows surrounded pools laid out behind the small casinos. While some of the larger casinos such as the MGM Grand and the Las Vegas Hilton did have towers and were not designed in the bungalow style, even these hotels attracted customers through neon lights, large marquees, and flashing bright lights.

When Steve Wynn sat on the hood of his car that day he envisioned a different Las Vegas, one filled with palm trees, tropical vegetation, and flaming rocks. While many of the casinos had names that suggested a theme, such as the Dunes, none had taken the theme concept to the level envisioned by Wynn. He suspected that if his casino looked like a scene from the South Pacific on the outside, it might just make people wonder what it looked like on the inside, and that would make people want to enter. Wynn wondered to himself what people's reactions would be when they saw this spectacle of greenery in the dessert. Would they, he questioned, think it was a mirage?

Wynn already owned the controlling interest in the Golden Nugget located in downtown Las Vegas. He used his success with the hotel casino to borrow $630 million—a figure unheard of at the time. Wynn approached his friend, Wall Street lender Michael Milken, and pitched his idea. Milken believed in Wynn's vision and issued junk bonds to fund the project. Wynn was so sure his idea would be a success that he entered into an agreement that would have sent most sound businessmen screaming away in panic. Wynn signed a seven-year loan for the money. This meant that Wynn's new property would have to bring in $1 million a day just to stay afloat. It was an incredible risk and caused many experienced casino executives to predict Wynn's downfall. "You can't make a nut of a million dollars a day with that set-up," one competing executive told a reporter. "The costs are enormous. Wynn's borrowed up to his eyeballs."

Wynn's plans for the property were enormous. He didn't intend to build another small Strip casino. The hotel had almost three thousand rooms, nearly three hundred of which were suites. The ample gaming area held over two thousand slot machines. There was a pool, a theater, wedding chapels, a spa, and a shopping mall. Wynn started the property with the working name the Golden Nugget of the Strip, but eventually changed it to The Mirage.

The name alone was the first start in the Las Vegas transformation. Most properties had a name followed by the words "hotel casino," for example the Sands Hotel Casino. Wynn knew that the title "hotel casino" did not portray the spirit he wanted for his property. The Mirage was no hotel casino. It had no neon lights or blinking bulbs. The Mirage was a "resort," and that is the name Wynn chose.

The Mirage Resort opened in November 1989. Most casinos at the time were either directly on Las Vegas Boulevard, called "the Strip," or in close proximity where they could easily be seen from the Strip. Wynn changed that with The Mirage. He wanted to both intrigue his guests and invite them to come in, so he placed his property back away from the Strip. He hid the hotel with hundreds of palm trees and tropical vegetation, which surrounded a large pond formed at the base of an active volcano. The volcano erupted every half hour. Guests watched as colored water and real fire spewed into the pond. A convenient viewing area was built in front of the volcano and people were encouraged to stop and watch the free show. The volcano alone was nothing like anything Las Vegas had seen before. It caused numerous traffic accidents as tourists stopped in the middle of the busy Las Vegas Boulevard to view the spectacle.

Tucked behind the volcano was the entrance to the resort. Moving walkways transported visitors from the sidewalk to the entrance.

Along the way Wynn's voice spoke of the wonders the eager guest was about to discover. Just inside the front doors guests found live white tigers roaming a glass-enclosed habitat built just for them. The tigers were part of the Siegfried and Roy magic show Wynn had hired as headliners. Further inside the casino was an atrium covered by a "beautifully crafted glass dome highlighted with gem-like crystals." Exotic foliage surrounded a bridge that led to the casino. The tropical theme reflected in the foliage outside the casino was carried throughout the inside as well.

Another major change Wynn created involved his casino cage, which was no cage at all. The casino cage was the place where guests performed all monetary transactions, such as exchanging chips for currency. The name "cage" was derived from the fact that the counters were covered with thick, although decorative, bars intended to discourage would-be thieves. Wynn knew that a cage would not send the resort message he worked so hard to create, so he made his cage look exactly the same as his reservations counter, open and inviting.

Another difference was the marquee outside the hotel. Wynn wanted his resort to stand out from the rest in every imaginable way. He also knew that to make money, money had to be spent and he wasn't afraid to do it. At the time most marquees used large plastic letters that were hooked to the signs to spell out their promotions. Large blinking light bulbs drew tourists' attention to the signs. Wynn chose a different type of sign. He was one of the first to use computer screens and graphics. The sign was different from everything else on the Strip and immediately commanded attention. Within a few years other resorts followed Wynn's lead and computerized signs became the standard in Las Vegas.

But even with all these changes, Wynn knew the true way to keep his new resort afloat—attract the high roller. While not advertised to the general public, Wynn spent approximately $24 million to build eight luxury villas that he used to attract people willing to gamble a million dollars or more at his resort. He called the villas "residences" and furnished them with authentic European art from the seventeenth, eighteenth, and nineteenth centuries. They had ten-foot-tall French doors, hand-loomed carpets, and crystal chandeliers. And to top it off, each villa had a private kitchen, complete with staff.

High rollers flocked to the property. Alan Feldman, vice president of the Mirage, suspected that there might be "a hundred players worldwide" who could bet the million dollars sought after by Wynn. However, after six weeks Wynn requested a printout of players who had wagered a million or more in the new resort. When Feldman held up the list, there were twenty names on each page and there were twenty pages. Contrary to the early predictions of many casino executives, The Mirage was profitable from the very first month. In fact, it brought in close to $200 million the first year.

Steve Wynn and The Mirage set a standard that all future resorts were held to. In just one year, his new resort attracted so many visitors that it replaced the Hoover Dam as the state's leading tourist attraction. The completion of The Mirage sparked a building boom up and down the Strip. It ushered in the end of the neon culture and the bright blinking lights that so marked the face of Las Vegas. Steve Wynn and the Mirage brought gaming and Las Vegas into the twentieth century.

PEPCON EXPLOSION

1988

On a warm day in May, the residents of Las Vegas went about their daily routines. People drove their cars to the store, cleaned their homes, served customers, and dealt cards. The day progressed just as any other day, but as noon approached, the valley was rocked with an explosion larger than the nuclear blasts of the 1950s.

On May 4, 1998, as the valley was just getting into the swing of things, a fire started in a waste barrel at the batch house of the Pacific Engineering Production Company of Nevada (PEPCON). Located only ten miles outside Las Vegas, the 1,500-acre plant was a producer of rocket fuel and one of only two producers of ammonium perchlorate, a chemical used to accelerate rocket fuel combustion. PEPCON was a regular supplier to NASA until the space shuttle *Columbia* disaster, which grounded all flights and eliminated the need for fuel to their rockets. However, it didn't stop the production of the chemical or of rocket fuel.

The ammonium perchlorate was located in an on-site storage facility. On that day in May there were more than six million pounds of ammonium perchlorate stored on site, enough to wipe out the entire town. While only a single barrel caught fire, the flames spread quickly across the plant. They headed toward the storage unit and threatened a gas pipeline, buried six feet underground, which ran across the entire facility.

PEPCON workers immediately fought the fire. Unfortunately they were armed with only garden-type water hoses and their efforts were futile. In the midst of the confusion, comptroller Roy Westerfield immediately recognized the seriousness of the situation. Instead of running away from the fire, he went to a phone and called for help. At 11:54 a.m. he contacted the fire department. "Emergency! We need the fire department! All you can get here!"

While Westerfield called for help, a loud explosion ripped across the plant. It was the first of three. "Everyone was curious as to what it was," recalled dockworker Joe Hedrick. "We didn't see any flames. In the past when we had a fire, it was handled." While the curious employees wondered what was happening, one supervisor, Bruce Halker, sensed something wasn't right and evacuated employees.

In the past, every emergency, no matter what type, had always been handled quickly and effectively by plant personnel and for this reason the employees didn't panic. That is until a second, larger explosion sent a shockwave across the grounds. The wave was so strong it sucked in the side of Hedrick's truck. The explosion sent a ball of fire high into the air, engulfed many of the buildings, and created a raging inferno. Confusion ensued at the plant and people started running for their lives.

"I was scared. I was really scared," recalled Clark County Fire Department captain Don Griffie, who responded to the fire. Griffie was concerned with the speed at which the fire spread. He knew that the fire had already gotten out of control and might just be unstoppable. Plus, as Griffie noticed when he arrived, "The closest fire hydrant was roughly one mile from the facility." His greatest fears came to pass only seconds later when the third explosion hit.

Unknown to the swarm of evacuees, the fire had reached the storage facility and the six million pounds of stored ammonium perchlorate. When the fire ignited the chemical, the blast was massive. It was so strong it pulled the pipeline completely out of the ground. When it hit, a bright flash lit the sky and a thick cloud of gray smoke climbed quickly upward. A shockwave immediately formed at the base of the cloud and spread swiftly across the desert floor. It completely decimated the building next to it, as if it were constructed of toothpicks.

The third explosion, which was comparable to 250 tons of dynamite, was strong enough to vaporize anyone in the immediate vicinity. "The explosion knocked me twelve feet in the air," recalled Griffie. "I was scared that I had possibly killed my crew." Workers ran as fast as they could in an attempt to outrun the shockwave, while pieces of flaming rubble flew over their heads. As the blast came, Jim Blackford, a firefighter from the Henderson Fire Department, rushed to the scene in a fire truck. The explosion was so strong it shattered the vehicle's windows. "It actually picked the truck up and moved it over two lanes. I looked over at my captain and his face was completely covered with blood," recalled Blackford.

Only a few miles from the PEPCON plant was a marshmallow factory, called Kidd & Company Marshmallows. An assistant manager, feeling the PEPCON explosion, looked out a window and saw the fireball as it moved toward the factory. He immediately got on the intercom and ordered the employees to evacuate. In a stroke of luck, the production line had been shut down that day. Had the line been up and running, the employees most likely would not have been able to hear their manager. This would have prevented them from getting out of the building before it was engulfed in flames.

The shockwave spread quickly into the surrounding community. "It looked like the whole earth was moving," recalled Griffie. Tiles buckled in local schools as terrified children hid under their desks. "We thought someone was out there with a shotgun," recalled Basic High School teacher Michael Neighbors. "Like fools, we went right for the windows." It proved to be a bad idea. The windows blew out. Shards of glass were sprayed in all directions and pieces were embedded into the walls. As the wave progressed, garage doors buckled, and cars were flipped over.

Ten miles away, the casinos along the Strip went about business as usual. While the blast was loud, the environment inside the casinos was even louder. This caused the blast to go largely unnoticed. The same was not true, however, for the quickly moving shockwave. When it reached the casinos, it blew out windows like they were made of sugar.

The blast registered 3.5 on the Richter scale. It was felt over seventy miles away in the town of Overton. "It was a loud roar, an enormous explosion; just unbelievable," recalled Griffie. As the wave spread, the concussion rang in people's ears. Many were rendered temporarily deaf. When the smoke finally cleared, metal buildings were found caved in and cars crushed. More than four hundred people were injured, but amazingly, only two had died: Roy Westerfield and Bruce Halker.

During the investigation it was determined that the waste barrel the fire started in contained a small amount of the ammonium perchlorate. The first explosion was the barrel igniting. It most likely blew through the building it was located in, soaring through the air and landing near the storage site of the ammonium perchlorate. The Clark County Fire Department determined that the fire in the barrel was caused by a welder's spark. But a separate investigator blamed it on a discarded cigarette. It was also determined that unsafe levels of hydrogen stored improperly may have contributed to all three blasts.

Reports estimated that the three blasts caused between $74 million and $300 million in damage to the valley. But there was some good news. Winds, not at all common to the valley, were in force that day. When the explosion occurred the winds managed to move the chemical away from populated areas into the unpopulated desert. Had that not happened the chemical residue would have fallen back to the ground to be absorbed in the soil. This, most likely, saved many lives. Because of the efforts of people like Westerfield and Halker, evacuations occurred quickly and many more deaths were avoided.

While PEPCON eventually moved to Utah, the scars on the ground where the site was located remain. So too do the scars of some of the people involved. "I dream about it," recalled Griffie. "I have nightmares about what happened every time I see that explosion on the T.V."

HELL ON THE STREETS

1992

A line of armed police officers fitted with riot gear formed a blockade at the intersection of Main and Bonanza. They stood in a line, side by side to form a human wall between a group of African-American youth and some of the oldest casinos on the famous Fremont Street in downtown Las Vegas. Reports had come in earlier to the Las Vegas Metropolitan Police Department (LVMPD) that the group was intent on burning the casinos to the ground.

The scene was sparked by a court ruling the day before and an event that had occurred almost a year earlier with no seeming connection to Las Vegas. On the afternoon of April 29, 1992, tension filled the air as jurors returned to their seats. The foreman handed the bailiff the paperwork containing the verdict to be read and pronounced by the court. Four Los Angeles police officers stood at the defendants' table. Their lawyers had worked hard to justify the actions of the officers against Rodney King, an African-American motorist the four stood accused of beating. Their hearts pounded as the judge studied the verdict. The trial had received national media attention not only for the racial issues associated with the incident, but also because the entire beating had been caught on videotape by an uninvolved bystander.

When the jury that consisted of ten Caucasians, one Latino, and one Asian handed their verdict to the judge, the threat of violence if another perceived injustice was handed down was almost more than the city could bear. At 3:15 p.m. the judge read the verdict, which acquitted three of the officers on all charges. The jury also stated that they could not come to a conclusion regarding one of the assault charges on the fourth officer—Lawrence Powell. They eventually returned a conviction on one count. The verdict almost immediately prompted a flare-up of violence and rioting that hadn't been seen since the Watts riots of 1965. Within two hours of the verdict, parts of Los Angeles were on fire.

When the residents of South Central Los Angeles rioted in the streets, the residents of Las Vegas took notice, especially those living in West Las Vegas, the mainly African-American–populated portion of town. On April 30, 1992, the second night of riots in Los Angeles, a group of African Americans gathered in West Las Vegas to hold what they described as a peaceful demonstration. The LVMPD were notified of the gathering and told that the group intended to burn down the casinos on Fremont Street. The police headed off the group at the intersection of Bonanza and Main, near downtown Las Vegas.

Police set up barricades to prevent the group from advancing and formed a human line of police officers. Lieutenant Steve Franks was in charge of the situation. He had been warned of the gathering and was told that the group had already damaged property. He was also informed that the group was intent on burning down the casinos. Franks was prepared to defend the city and stop the group at all costs. "Had it not been for our officers," recalled Franks, "this town would have gone up in flames."

At around 7:30 p.m. the crowd reached the barricade of police officers. They were ordered to stop their gathering and return to their homes by Franks. The crowd did not take well to being stopped and did not respond to the order. The crowd grew increasingly boisterous. Chants of freedom and judicial injustice were hurled at the police officers from the increasingly impatient crowd. It was clear to Franks that the group had no intention of backing down. The police were well aware of the riots occurring in Los Angeles and they were concerned that this group would follow their lead. Faced with no other way to avoid a physical confrontation, the police made the decision to use tear gas to disperse the crowd. The tear gas worked and the crowd cleared the area. Although the crowd had left, thoughts of riots lingered and the police were determined to show a strong force. They barricaded West Las Vegas from the rest of the city and refused to let anyone in or out.

That same night in the Garson Park projects two gangs gathered to iron out a truce. The Bloods and Crips had called a truce in Los Angeles and their Las Vegas counterparts followed suit. A LVMPD patrol car saw the gathering and drove into the crowd. The group scattered, but returned quickly. They threw rocks and bottles at the vehicle as the officers inside called for backup. At some point shots were fired and the gang members ran away.

A short distance away another group gathered and started a riot. They threw rocks into the glass storefronts of many local businesses and gas stations. Others entered the buildings and took whatever they could carry. A group went to a nearby office of the Parole and Pardon Board. They threw a Molotov cocktail into the window and burnt the building to the ground. Businesses were damaged and destroyed with no regard to who owned or operated them. A struggling, mainly African-American–owned shopping center, called Nucleus Plaza, was torched and all but destroyed. Even the local headquarters of the

National Association for the Advancement of Colored People was destroyed in the scuffle.

Looting was rampant and anyone unlucky enough to be found in the area was beaten. A forty-nine-year-old immigrant from Czechoslovakia was on his way to his job as a security officer when his car was attacked by a mob of more than one hundred people. They kicked out his windows, pulled him from his car, and beat him severely. "They pulled me to the ground, punching, kicking. They were pushing each other out of the way, each competing to get to hit me." When a break in the beating occurred, the security officer was able to climb back into his car. He drove through the crowd, which continued to batter and beat his car, until he was spotted by a group of police officers. He told the officers that the mob told him they were beating him because he was white.

The riots continued through the night. Buildings and homes were destroyed and police officers were fired upon. One police officer described the scene as "hell on the streets." When the night gave way to day the riots ended. But as soon as the night returned, so too did the riots. They continued for sixteen of the next eighteen days, with only two nights of relative peace.

Fear spread not only through West Las Vegas, but through most of the valley as well. The police did their best to try and calm the residents but many business owners armed themselves to protect their property. The African-American community gathered together and called for the rioting to stop. Some of the leaders blamed the riots on gang members who, they claimed, used the Rodney King verdict as an excuse to riot under the cause of social injustice. "These are people that don't even care about the Rodney King verdict. They are terrorizing our community. And we want them stopped."

The riots did eventually stop. Unfortunately by the time they did, the property damage totaled more than $6 million and one police officer was wounded by gunfire. Amazingly the riots claimed the life of only one person—an eighteen-year-old man who was burned in a building he reportedly entered to loot.

In the end, the riots served to open the eyes of the community to the plight of the struggling area. Mayor Jan Laverty Jones reported to the *Las Vegas Sun,* a local newspaper, "I think the riots raised everyone's awareness about a problem that had been there and that no one was doing anything about. People said, 'Pay attention,' and we did."

Before the riots the area of West Las Vegas held a close resemblance to the area of South Central Los Angeles. In the months and years since the riots, West Las Vegas was rebuilt with the help of some very prominent personalities including boxer Sugar Ray Leonard and basketball great Earvin "Magic" Johnson. A five-year job replacement plan, called Nevada Partners, was created. A middle school was reopened and a branch of the Bank of America opened on Martin Luther King Boulevard. The police, criticized by the African-American community for the way they handled the incident, made great strides to reduce racial tension and increase a positive relationship with the community.

GANG MEMBERS TERRORIZE
THE STRIP

1994

On a cool May morning, a black pickup truck pulled in front of the Sands Hotel and Casino. Two men jumped from the bed of the truck armed with shotguns. Another climbed out of the driver's side and slammed the door behind him. The three men pulled ski masks over their faces, stormed into the casino, and headed straight for the casino cage. When they arrived one of the men cocked his shotgun and pointed it at the security officer sitting at the elevated podium. The other two jumped over the counter of the cage and ordered the cashiers to fill bags with money. The scared employees stuffed money into the bags while the robbers held weapons to their heads and berated them. When the bags were filled, the men leapt back over the counter and the three left as quickly as they came. The entire incident took less than ninety seconds. It was a picture perfect robbery. Except that this robbery was staged, and the men who pulled it off were the police.

Las Vegas had seen a rash of robberies. In the past nineteen months, seven casinos had been robbed in the same manner as the police pretended to rob the Sands. Only these robberies were real. They weren't filmed for training purposes, as was the incident at the Sands. In these robberies, real weapons were used, real people were involved, and real money was stolen. The town was up in arms. The robberies had received national attention and city officials were concerned not only with catching the criminals but also the effect the robberies had on tourism.

It all started one early November morning in 1992 when four masked men stormed into the San Remo Hotel Casino and invaded the casino cage. The men were heavily armed and they caught the cage employees unprepared. Frightened cashiers filled pillowcases with cash and handed them over to the bandits, who quickly escaped. While the entire incident was caught on surveillance cameras, the police had few clues to go by. Although the town was shocked, the incident was viewed more as a one-time occurrence than the beginning of a streak that would terrorize employees and tourists alike.

The masked bandits hit the San Remo a second time on August 28, 1993. On this occasion, the robbery didn't go as smoothly. To get the attention of the employees and the guests playing at the table games and slot machines, the bandits fired four shots into the air, blowing holes in the ceiling. Stunned guests hit the floor and terror filled the air. "They're going in heavily armed. They're not concerned about being involved in a shootout," reported Lieutenant Mike Hawkins of the Las Vegas Metropolitan Police Department. As the bandits rushed to the cage, one of them stopped and held a shotgun to the head of an unarmed security officer. The frightened officer remained motionless as the terrified cashiers again filled pillowcases with cash.

City officials were outraged and security was baffled. "It never happened before," recalled Sands chief of security and former San Diego police officer John Murray. "We never had a casino robbed."

About six months later, on February 22, the bandits struck again at the Aladdin Hotel and Casino. Five masked men entered the casino through a side entrance and rushed to the casino cage. Instead of firing shots, the men waved shotguns at the guests and yelled out to the stunned players who immediately took refuge behind slot machines and under gaming tables. Just as they did at the San Remo, the group attacked the cage and ordered the employees to fill pillowcases. The robbery took less than two minutes and when it was over the group left in a van. Once again the incident was all caught on security and surveillance tapes. But most importantly for the police, the van was caught on tape as well. It was recovered a short time later.

Shortly after the San Remo incident the Federal Bureau of Investigation (FBI) received a tip about one of the people possibly involved in the casino robbery. "Tourism is the lifeblood of Las Vegas," recalled a spokesman for the Las Vegas FBI office. "Anytime something tarnishes the reputation that this is a fun place to bring your families, alarm bells ring." The tip led the FBI to Los Angeles and a sixteen-year-old gang member who was arrested and charged with two counts of attempted murder and robbery with a deadly weapon in connection with the San Remo robbery.

The FBI formed a theory. They believed that the robberies were being carried out and masterminded by one or more Los Angeles gangs. This theory was bolstered when the van recovered from the Aladdin robbery was linked to Los Angeles gang members.

Las Vegas had allowed itself to become a prime target for these invasion-type robberies. Corporations had moved organized crime out of Las Vegas and had taken over. When the Mob ran the town, money was the main concern and they controlled the flow of money with a heavy hand. No one in their right mind would ever consider robbing a Mob-owned casino, for retribution would be swift and complete. The casinos were also more protected in those days. Bars placed over the counters of the casino cages (giving them their name) served as a barrier between the guest and the money. Security officers were armed and expected to use those weapons if a situation occurred.

All that changed when corporations took over Las Vegas. Starting with Steve Wynn's Mirage, the bars were removed from the casino cages. Wynn not only took the weapons away from security, he also took them out of their uniforms and placed them in softer, more guest-friendly clothing. Other casinos followed. Nevada gaming laws also required that the casino have enough cash on hand to cover the chips on the floor or in the cage. This often meant that during or immediately after big events, the casino had a great deal of cash on hand. Having a large amount of cash, with no bars on the cages, was a recipe for disaster. "This is going to continue . . . as long as we leave cash lying out there like candy," stated Gold Coast security chief Beecher Avants.

The directors and chiefs of security met to tackle the situation. While they understood the corporate desire to make the guest feel comfortable, they also knew the importance of protection and, more importantly, deterrence. Many felt that it was no coincidence that the robbers had only struck casinos with unarmed security and that they had avoided those casinos where the security officers were still armed. The police also understood the situation that security was in. "The hotels are in a Catch-22. If they build them to be robbery-safe, they'd be like fortresses and unattractive to tourists." Casinos that had armed security stepped up its visibility on the Strip. Casinos like the Sands made sure an armed security officer was in front of the property at all times. The move was designed as much to comfort guests as it was to deter the robbers.

The robberies finally came to a head when two casinos were robbed in three days. On Friday April 22, 1994, the masked bandits struck again. This time they hit the Flamingo Hotel and Casino. As before, the men came in heavily armed and left with almost

$150,000. Two days later the same group robbed Harrah's. At 2:45 a.m. four masked men stormed the casino, armed to the teeth, and headed straight for the casino cage. Just as had happened every time, guests dove under games and security was held at bay with shotguns. A fifth man waited in a van outside the casino. When the four men left the casino with close to $100,000, they jumped into the van and yelled at the fifth man to hit the gas.

As is always the case in Las Vegas, the odds caught up with the men when lady luck turned her head the other way. The men drove a short distance and then abandoned the van. They switched to a second van they had stolen earlier and continued their escape. As the second van approached Koval Lane, a short distance away from Harrah's, a police officer spotted it. The van had already been reported stolen and the officer recognized it from a broadcast description. The officer hit his lights. The driver of the van saw the lights and sped off. The chase was on.

The van led the police on a twenty-minute race throughout the town. At one point a police officer saw an opportunity to cut off the van. The officer sped up and pulled his patrol car in front of the van. Once in front he hit his brakes. The van rammed the patrol car. The impact sent the car into an uncontrolled swerve. The bandits flew by as the patrol car slammed into a fire hydrant. As the bandits raced away, they attempted to discard their weapons. They were only able to get rid of one handgun when they passed a mall. Luckily it was recovered before the mall, a local youth hangout, opened for business.

The men in the van continued their escape. They rammed every police vehicle that got in front of them and sent another into a light pole. Luckily, the incident occurred in the early morning when the streets were relatively deserted. As the van approached Topaz and Russell Road, the police were presented with one more opportunity to cut the van off. This time it worked.

Excited police exited their vehicles and quickly drew their weapons, using their patrol cars as protection. They knew these men were heavily armed and they took no chances. Tensions rose as the police wondered if the men would choose a Bonnie and Clyde–type shootout instead of surrendering peacefully. They ordered the men to exit the van, and as the door of the van slid open, the officers sighted in on the suspects. When the five men exited the van, hands in the air, the police approached cautiously, canine units at their side. They ordered the men to lie face down on the ground and let their canine counterparts hover over them to deter any thoughts the men might have of trying to run. The five men were taken into custody, but when the van was searched, no money was found.

The capture of the five men marked the end of the robberies that terrorized the Las Vegas casinos. All of the men involved were arrested and convicted. Many of them were teenagers who were tried as adults and given lengthy prison terms (the sixteen-year-old in the San Remo incident was sentenced to thirty years). Two Los Angeles gang members were arrested as the masterminds of the incidents and were each sentenced to twenty-two years in jail. After the Harrah's robbery many casinos replaced the bars in their cages (although they eventually removed them). The police also developed a training program, the one filmed at the Sands, and used it to train all security and police. However, the best tool against robberies proved to be the silent alarms installed in many casinos that linked them directly to the police department.

THE ONE HUNDRED YEAR FLOOD

1999

July promised to be another scorcher in the Las Vegas valley. One hundred degree–plus temperatures were common for that time of year and were reached without much encouragement. While July had started out hot, rain was forecast for the 8th. Television weather personalities warned that the conditions were ripe for an intense rainfall. But the hardened residents of Las Vegas had heard it all before. They were used to seeing gray clouds form, only to have them blown into Arizona or Utah without leaving so much as a drop of rain. So when at 10:30 a.m. gray thunderclouds moved into the valley and rain came pouring down, the residents of Las Vegas weren't initially alarmed. But, when the rain came down harder and lasted longer than normal, it became quickly apparent that this was no typical Las Vegas storm.

The high areas noticed it first. Rain poured down hard and gathered quickly. It formed deep fast-moving rivers that rushed past houses and buildings into the streets toward the many natural washes in the valley. Gravity soon took over and the rain gained momentum.

As the rain moved it built in force. It carried objects with it and destroyed everything in its path. People were stranded in their vehicles and portions of the town were completely shut down.

Unfortunately 294 days of sunshine a year tend to make the Earth's crust a little hard, and hard crust does not absorb water well. Added to the hard-baked ground was the fact that one of the main sediments in the valley was calcium carbonate. Long before the residents of Las Vegas moved into the valley, water had mixed with calcium carbonate to form a rock-like structure called caliche. As hard as concrete and almost completely impervious to water, the layer of caliche under the soil turned the ground into a giant water slide. Instead of being able to absorb the water as it passed, the hard ground only contributed to its speed and force.

The water moved swiftly from the highlands to the lower valley, which was also battered in a heavy sheet of rain. It poured into the Flamingo Wash, which couldn't hold the one and a half to three inches per hour that fell. By noon the street in front of Caesars Palace had become an impromptu lake. Water levels rose above the tires of many cars. The flooding continued and water poured into the famous fountains at the casino's entrance. Caesars Palace was directly in the path of the water flow to the Flamingo Wash. The rain rushed through a rear service entrance and made its way into the casino, flooding a card pit. The Forum Shopping Mall inside Caesars Palace was forced to close to stop the rush of water that had already reached several of the shops.

Water levels rose as high as fourteen feet in some areas. Tourists and residents alike didn't know how to react. They were advised to stay off the streets and sidewalks. Many casinos canceled shows and closed pools. New York-New York Hotel and Casino closed its Manhattan Express rollercoaster and the Stratosphere closed its tower. McCarran International Airport shut down for forty-five minutes. In that time, two planes were diverted to Los Angeles and one to Phoenix before the rain slowed enough to allow landing to resume.

As the waters rushed across the street from Caesars Palace, the first floor of the parking structure under the Imperial Palace become a raging river as 4.5 billion gallons of rushing water raced through the garage into the Flamingo Wash. The rush of water was so intense it widened the channel in the wash by as much as three hundred feet in many places. Fear of accidental drowning became a reality. The Las Vegas Metropolitan Police Department acted quickly. They placed barricades to block off the area and brought vehicle and pedestrian traffic to a complete stop. Unfortunately when the waters finally did subside, the body of a homeless man was pulled from the wash. Unable to escape the raging river of water, he became entangled in a tree and drowned.

It wasn't like Las Vegas hadn't imagined that a flood like this could occur. In fact, in the years before the flood, Clark County had planned the creation of many catch basins designed to assist in the event of just such a flash flood. Unfortunately the planning came too late and only two basins were finished when the rains of 1999 fell. As the water poured into the finished basins, one area of town took a particularly bad hit. The Miracle Mile Mobile Home Park was positioned near the wetlands in an area next to the Flamingo Wash. Natural washes channeled almost the entire force of the rain into the wetlands exactly where the mobile home park waited. As billions of gallons of water flowed over the walls of the basin, it instantly eroded the banks. The park became a victim of rising waters and forceful erosion. The metal homes were no match for the raging waters. It pulled them from their foundations into the fast-moving water like they were made of paper. At least three of the homes were swept entirely into the wash. They were completely destroyed as the waters carried them away.

As the news of the damage reached the residents of Las Vegas, many businesses closed and employees were allowed to go home. Makeshift shelters were created in many schools and several casinos provided shelter and food to tourists and residents alike. Just as quickly as the water came, national news also flooded the area. They broadcast film of houses succumbing to raging waters and motorists forced to the roofs of their cars by the rising waters, desperate for the police or fire department to arrive.

Rain started at 10:30 that morning and didn't stop until almost 4:30 that evening. When the rain finally stopped, it left a disaster in its wake. Governor Kenny Guinn flew to Las Vegas and surveyed the area from a helicopter. "It's a wide strip of devastation," Guinn said. Mayor Oscar Goodman viewed the affected area firsthand and called it a tragedy. When the effects of the damage were counted it totaled more than $20.5 million with $5 million of that to the flood control system. More than 360 homes and countless vehicles were damaged or destroyed.

The Clark County Fire Department and the Las Vegas Metropolitan Police Department received 1,262 emergency calls between the hours of 10:30 a.m. and 4:00 p.m.—677 more than normal for that time period. They went on approximately 130 rescue calls, most of which were from stranded motorists who were either caught unaware by the rain, or who had foolishly ventured into the raging waters, pitting machine against nature—with the machine falling woefully short. Rain flooded the interstate, motorists were stranded, and cars damaged.

Although the damage to property was severe, the loss of life was minimal. Only two people died as a result of the flooding, the homeless man caught in the wash and a ninety-one-year-old woman who was unable to stop her car when she hit the flood waters and crashed into another vehicle. While only two basins were complete, one of them allowed enough water to pass that it saved a nursing home and a home for the mentally disabled from severe damage.

The likelihood of a rainstorm the magnitude of the one that happened on July 8, 1999 occurring in the next one hundred years is only 1 percent. While that may have been considered a safe bet before the 1999 flood, it's likely that none of the residents of Las Vegas would take that bet again.

TIGER ATTACK ON THE STRIP

2003

When Roy Horn walked toward the audience on October 3, 2003, a little after 8:00 p.m., he probably wasn't thinking about the more than five thousand performances he and his partner Siegfried had completed. Most likely he was running the lines for the bit he was about to perform through his head. It was his job to convince the capacity crowd that the seven-year-old royal white tiger by his side had never stepped on stage before this night. Of course, it wasn't true; Montecore had been a regular part of the act since he was six months old.

For many in the audience, it was the first time they had been so close to an actual tiger, never mind a rare royal white. Just as he had done so often before, Roy told the excited audience "this is his first time on stage." The tiger was supposed to perform at Roy's command, astounding the audience at how quickly the big cat learned. While some audience members were fooled, the line was really meant as more of a joke and this portion of the act was a lighthearted section intended to show the white tiger up close. But Montecore had another idea. Almost as soon as Roy gave Montecore the command to lie down, the tiger clamped its large teeth onto Roy Horn's arm.

Roy Horn and Siegfried Fischbacher were both born in Germany, five years apart and in separate towns. The two met on a cruise ship where Roy worked as a waiter and Siegfried as a cabin steward. Siegfried had always shown an interest in magic and illusions and he could often be found performing magic tricks for the guests. When the directors of the cruise line took notice, Siegfried translated those tricks into his own show.

Roy's interests did not lie with magic. Instead he had a strong interest in exotic animals. On one trip, Roy smuggled a cheetah named Chico on board the cruise ship. When Siegfried saw the animal, thoughts of working it into his show wrestled around in his head and that night, the act known as Siegfried and Roy was born.

Siegfried and Roy started their Las Vegas run at the Tropicana in 1967, moving to the Stardust and eventually the Frontier where they received the Show of the Year award in 1972. Their fame, however, didn't launch until Mirage CEO Steve Wynn lured the pair with a showroom built exclusively for them and an estimated paycheck of more than $57 million a year. In 2000 they were elected magicians of the century by the brotherhood of magic's International Magicians Society. They were the most famous illusionists in Las Vegas. The Mirage even had a statue tribute built for their star performers on the Las Vegas Strip. Ironically, the statue served as a photo opportunity for tourists, who placed their bodies inside the open mouth of the tiger included in the sculpture.

The pair concentrated Roy's love for exotic animals into a passion to save the royal white tiger. They made the animals a large part of their act and Wynn built a garden paradise for them on Mirage property. Siegfried and Roy's passion for exotic animals did not stop when they exited the showroom doors. All of the animals in the show lived with the pair at their home in Las Vegas. They had thirty-eight white tigers, twenty-three white lions, and a handful of various other large cats. The animals roamed the grounds freely and it was not at all uncommon to see Roy where he was happiest—with his cats out on the grounds. Roy once said of his legacy, "If anything, I'd like to be remembered as the man who gave back the magic white lions and white tigers."

Siegfried and Roy created illusions with a Liberace flair, complete with flamboyant costumes and outstanding special effects. That night when Roy Horn stepped on stage he was celebrating his fifty-ninth birthday. His official party had been held the night before, in the same theater. He had more than six hundred of his friends and fans in attendance and it had placed Roy in a good mood. He was still in that mood when he gave Montecore the command to lie down. However, instead of lying down, the tiger took a playful pat at Roy's arm, which prompted a roar of laughter from the audience.

The pat caused Roy to drop the chain leash connected to the tiger's neck. When he reached to take hold of it, Montecore clamped his jaws on the performer's arm. With the tiger's teeth embedded in his arm, Roy was left with no choice but to get the big cat's attention. He hit the tiger on the head with the only weapon at his disposal— the microphone he held in his free hand. "He started beating the tiger with his microphone," recalled a tourist from Miami, seated close to the stage, "and the next thing I know, Siegfried is running across the stage yelling, 'No, no, no!'."

Montecore did let go, but only long enough to lunge at Roy, taking hold of his neck. While many of the audience may have thought that Montecore's biting of Roy's arm was part of the show, when the tiger took hold of Roy's neck, the more than 1,500 people in the audience knew that something had gone terribly wrong. "There were a couple of gasps, and people thought it was part of the act, and then it was real quiet," recalled one audience member. "When it grabbed him and dragged him off the stage, I thought maybe it was like some magic trick where they switch a rag doll or something," recalled another. The audience quickly realized that the scene they had just witnessed was not part of the show. "A lady ran past me freaking out and it was then I sort of, in the back of my mind, thought now this isn't part of the show," recalled an audience member from Australia.

Montecore dragged Roy off stage followed by a security officer and two stagehands. Many of the audience described the scene the same way. "It literally drug him by his neck off the stage like a rag doll," recalled one audience member. "He looked like a rag doll in his mouth," recalled another. When Roy was taken behind the curtain it did nothing to control the growing fears of the audience members. "We just heard all this commotion behind the curtain and you could hear Roy scream," recalled one woman. "Everyone at our table was kind of looking at each other, like 'Oh my God.'"

Mirage security was immediately contacted and emergency services were dispatched to the hotel at 8:21 p.m. They arrived four minutes later at 8:25 p.m. The stunned audience was still recovering when a visibly shaken Siegfried returned to the stage about five minutes after the attack. In a shaky voice he apologized to the audience and told them that the show needed to be canceled. As he walked off stage, the lights came on and the crowd slowly left the showroom. Many were in shock—they just shook their heads as they walked— while others cried.

When the Clark County Fire Department (CCFD) arrived on scene they found Roy Horn in bad shape. He had suffered from severe blood loss, but fortunately was still breathing. They loaded Roy into the ambulance as quickly as possible and sped off to the closest hospital. On the trip to the hospital Roy fought the paramedics' attempts to insert a tube into his throat to help him breathe.

"He was fighting them, which is a good thing because that means he could breathe on his own," recalled a representative from the CCFD. In the ambulance Roy was conscious, although he did have trouble breathing, and complained about how his throat hurt. Strangely enough, it was fortunate that the incident happened in Las Vegas and not another town in the state, because the hospital Roy was rushed to had the only Level 1 trauma center in Nevada.

The news of Roy's accident swept through the town and local celebrities arrived at the hospital almost as soon as the ambulance. Fellow magician Lance Burton was one of the first to arrive. "I saw Roy just last night at his birthday party. You just hate for anything like this to happen to anyone. You just hope for the best." Many celebrities on the Strip sympathized with Roy. They worked with wild animals as well and they understood the dangers associated with having animals in their act. "Whenever you work with animals it's a risk," recalled Frankie Scinta, a member of a family of entertainers. "It's an unfortunate mishap, but they will bounce back. They're royalty in Las Vegas." Although his friends remained hopeful, Roy was not doing well.

The tiger was immediately quarantined and an investigation began. The investigation initially focused on the handling of the big cats and the possibility that Montecore was simply hungry. However, that was quickly proved to be incorrect. In the end no one was ever able to say definitively why Montecore attacked Roy on that night. Roy survived the attack. It left him partially paralyzed but with full comprehension and speech. Roy fought hard to defend Montecore and was the driving force behind saving the animal's life. Siegfried and Roy remained active in their quest to save the white tigers and lions. On February 28, 2009 Siegfried and Roy—with Montecore by their side—appeared once more on stage, doing a brief performance for a charity.

A BRITISH BATTLESHIP
BLOWS UP THE DUNES

2003

A British captain stood erect on the deck of a British battleship in the cool Las Vegas night. His blue military uniform was topped with a tall hat complete with a thick white plume. He faced the south where a pirate ship lay helplessly in port directly in front of him. In his right hand he held a gleaming sword with tassels that hung from the handle. The moonlight caught the blade when he lifted the weapon high in the air. In an instant he pulled the sword swiftly to his side, signaling the cannon master who fired the main cannon. Thick white smoke escaped from the barrel of the cannon. But the target wasn't the defenseless pirate ship; it was the Dunes Hotel and Casino.

Las Vegas is known for its glitz and showmanship, but on October 27, 2003, even Vegas was surprised with the Hollywood-style destruction of one of its oldest landmarks. The Dunes Hotel and Casino was built in 1955 and opened on May 23 of that year. Even before it was built, the Dunes attracted headlines. Rumored to be funded by the Mafia, the Dunes was reported to have been built using $3.5 million from the Teamsters' pension fund. While the rumor sparked an initial interest in the resort, the 194-room resort struggled after its opening. The main problem was that the owners of the hotel had chosen a terrible place to put the new hotel. Instead of placing it near other casinos, the Dunes was located so far away from the rest of the casinos that it went largely unnoticed. Although it billed itself as "the world's friendliest casino," even the chairman of the board, Frank Sinatra—on loan from the Sands— couldn't revive the Dunes' sagging revenues.

But there was hope on the horizon, hope in the form of a vice. Although gambling was already a mainstay in Las Vegas, in 1955 the area hadn't yet reached its status of Sin City. The owners of the Dunes had a plan to bring in patrons. They knew that people needed a reason to come to their casino—a reason that was more than just gambling—and that was what they intended to give them. On January 10, 1957, the Dunes opened the town's first topless review. While the town and the state didn't take well to the move, *Minsky's Follies* set attendance records and brought the struggling hotel to the status of a major player on the Strip.

In 1964 the Dunes again made headlines, sparking what would soon become a Las Vegas standard—extravagance, or as many would say, gaudiness. To emphasize the hotel's theme, the owners of the Dunes contracted to build a thirty-five-foot fiberglass sultan. When he was complete, they stood him, hands on hips, at the front entrance of the hotel. But the hotel also had its classier side. In 1967 a second tower was built on the property, which made the Dunes the largest and nicest hotel on the Strip. It also had one of only two golf courses on the Las Vegas Strip and the course was considered by many as the best in Las Vegas.

In 1992 when the hotel was sold to the developer and casino mogul Steve Wynn, it had fallen on hard times. The sultan was long gone. It had been moved years earlier to the golf course and had been destroyed in a fire. The hotel had been purchased five years earlier by a Japanese investor who simply could not make a go of it. In 1987 the Japanese investor paid a reported $155 million. In 1992 Wynn paid $57 million.

Wynn saw a gold mine in the property, but knew that before that gold could be mined, the Dunes needed to be destroyed. Demolitions in Las Vegas had always been a subtle event, largely taking place at night while the residents of the town slept. Wynn had a different idea. At the time Las Vegas was booming, four thousand people a month were moving into the area, thirty-five million tourists were visiting every year, and Wynn knew just how to get their attention. The Dunes was a Las Vegas landmark, and he decided to televise its implosion.

Wynn was a master showman. He intended to build his flagship property on the spot where the Dunes stood. He was also a man who understood the power of anticipation. All he had to do was generate excitement about his new property and people would want to come when it was finally built. Wynn used the implosion of the Dunes to generate the excitement he needed. He made the implosion a big deal. He invited Las Vegas society and gave them a show that they would never forget.

The spectacle was planned months before the event. Charges were placed at strategic places throughout the original twenty-three-story hotel tower, the casino, and even the old neon sign. The charges were designed both for function and for show. Wynn sent out invitations to the mayor and other dignitaries of Las Vegas, all of whom came. Wynn also contacted the three local television stations and convinced them to televise the event, something unheard of at that time.

Bleachers, used to seat the dignitaries invited to watch the event, were set up across the street from the Dunes. The public was welcome, but were kept away from the area by chain-link fences. An estimated 200,000 people showed up to the event and were treated to a large fireworks display shot from the top of the soon-to-be-imploded tower. The show brought cheers from the crowd.

Wynn, as he did with all of his properties, emceed the event. To generate even more excitement, he came across the speaker system and warned people with health problems to stand further away from the site. He assured the crowd that the spectacle would be safe, but very loud, and told them to "have a good time."

Further down the Strip, Wynn owned two casinos: the tropical-themed Mirage and the pirate-themed Treasure Island. While the two properties stood next to each other, they were designed to attract different crowds. At the time, the Mirage was the flagship of Wynn's Mirage Resorts Inc. It was fancy, sleek, and catered to the wealthy. The Treasure Island, on the other hand, was designed to attract the average gambler who wanted to have fun in a themed environment. Its chandeliers were made of simulated human bones, as were the handles on the entrance doors. The inside of the casino was designed to resemble the inside of a pirate ship, and the outside of the hotel, directly on the Strip, was the dock.

It was on this dock that a British warship, the HMS *Britannia,* fought a pirate ship in nightly duels. Every hour and a half nightly the ship patrolled the area. It came into port, spied the pirate ship, and engaged it in combat. The HMS *Britannia* never won any of the battles, but after all, it was a pirate port.

On October 27, 2003, at approximately 10:00 p.m., Wynn stepped onto the podium set up in front of the grandstand and ordered the HMS *Britannia* to fire its port cannons at the Dunes. The captain gave the order to fire and the ship obliged. When the cannons fired, the crowd was left to imagine cannonballs traveling through the air, south, down the Strip toward the Dunes.

The imaginary cannonballs hit their marks and fire exploded from the roof of the casino. Loud blasts shot up smoke and flames, which were meant to imitate the hits of each individual cannonball. When the first explosion hit, the crowd cheered loudly. The neon sign went next. Wynn kept it lit, and when the sign was struck by the imaginary cannonballs, fire shot skyward. The blasts were so powerful that they caused an unplanned fire to start on the asphalt roof of the casino. In no time the roof was engulfed in a bright blaze of orange flames, made more significant by the dark night sky. Within seconds the tower crumbled. Huge clouds of gray smoke filled the air and the excited crowd cheered loudly. The entire implosion, from the moment the cannonballs hit the casino until the tower collapsed, took less than ten minutes.

While Wynn planned the event to the last detail, he was unable to factor in Mother Nature. When the tower collapsed, the wind picked up. It pushed a wall of thick gray smoke into the crowd that quickly engulfed spectators and tourists alike. As the cloud continued a slow creep down the Strip, it covered everything in its path. The dark sky became darker and the Strip disappeared. The only visible indications that the rest of Las Vegas still existed were the neon signs of the other casinos on the Strip. The bright colors cut through the smoke, almost as an honor to a fallen comrade.

When the smoke finally dissipated, it left a skim of gray dust on the buildings and cars in the area. The remaining tower was brought down a few days later to much less fanfare and reduced media coverage. The event sparked a trend in Las Vegas to implode the old and bring in the new. Some of the implosions were used in movies such as *Con Air,* while others were just scheduled events, covered by the local media. From 1993 to 2007 fifteen hotels, casinos, and parts of hotels were demolished in true Las Vegas fashion to make way for the new.

LAS VEGAS FACTS AND TRIVIA

- The average temperature in Las Vegas is 66.3 degrees Fahrenheit, the average yearly rainfall is 4.13 inches, and there are 211 clear days each year.

- Almost forty million people visit Las Vegas every year, 81 percent have visited at least once before, and 84 percent of all visitors gamble. Those visitors spend more than $40 billion in Las Vegas every year.

- In 2004, Fremont Street (part of the old Boulder Highway) was closed to traffic. The street was turned into a walkway and covered by a $17 million canopy that extends the length of more than five football fields. Approximately 12.5 million LED modules create high-resolution images and special effects in nightly shows above the heads of tourists.

- Vegas Vic, the enormous neon cowboy that towers over Fremont Street, is the world's largest mechanical neon sign. When the Fremont Street Experience was being built, Vegas Vic and Sassy Sally, the neon cowgirl sign that lived across the street, were lowered and married by a local minister. Sally dutifully changed her name to Vegas Vicki.

- Las Vegas is home to more than seven hundred churches and synagogues, representing more than forty different faiths.

- A marriage license costs $55 in Nevada. There are 192 wedding chapels in Las Vegas, which perform between 110,000 and 130,000 weddings each year. Valentine's Day is the busiest day.

- Clark Country has 1,956 gaming licenses. There are more than 190,000 slot machines and around 5,500 live table games including poker.

- The MGM Grand has the largest gambling space at 171,500 square feet.

- All Las Vegas video slot machines must pay back a minimum of 75 percent on average according to state law. Even with the law, Clark County casinos take in more than $9 billion in gaming revenue every year.

- The largest slot machine payoff was $39.7 million. It occurred in March 2003, at the Excalibur Hotel Casino. A twenty-five-year-old man played only $100 before hitting the jackpot.

- The first modern high-rise on the Las Vegas Strip was the nine-story Riviera Hotel, which opened in 1955.

- Currently, seventeen of the twenty biggest hotels in the United States are in Las Vegas. There are 132,947 hotel rooms, almost ten thousand of which are in the four casinos located on the corner of Las Vegas Boulevard and Tropicana.

- The average room rate in Las Vegas is $132 a night and rooms are occupied more than 90 percent of the time.

- Almost three hundred movies have been filmed entirely or partially in Las Vegas, including: *The Mexican, Lethal Weapon 4, Ocean's Eleven* (both versions), *Con Air, Independence Day, Showgirls, Casino, Bugsy, Fools Rush In, Rocky III, The Godfather Part II, Austin Powers: International Man of Mystery, Rain Man,* and, of course, *Viva Las Vegas.*

- The Las Vegas convention facilities together have more than five million square feet of space. There are more than twenty-four thousand conventions each year with over six million people in attendance.

- On July 5, 1946, Norma Jean Dougherty took advantage of Nevada's liberal divorce laws (a person only has to be a resident for six weeks before filing for divorce) and divorced her husband James Edward Dougherty while he was away at sea. Norma Jean would eventually change her name to Marilyn Monroe.

- The famous "Strip" got its name from former Los Angeles police captain Guy McAfee, who claimed the road reminded him of the Sunset Strip between Hollywood and Beverly Hills.

- When it opened in October 1942, The Last Frontier transported guests from the airport to the hotel in an authentic stagecoach.

- The Stratosphere Tower is the tallest free-standing observation tower in the United States at 1,149 feet. It is also the tallest building in the state of Nevada and the tallest tower west of the Mississippi River.

- *Insanity the ride,* at the top of the Stratosphere Tower, is the highest thrill ride in the United States. It extends riders sixty-four feet over the end of the tower, above the observation deck, and spins them at a force of three Gs. Another ride at the top of the tower, *The Big Shot,* shoots passengers 160 feet upward at forty-five miles per hour, providing the highest view available of the Las Vegas Strip without flying.

- Before embarking on his political career, Ronald Reagan had a stage show in Las Vegas in the 1950s.

- New-York New-York Hotel Casino was flooded with memorabilia after the 9-11 bombings of the World Trade Center towers. It eventually turned the memorabilia into a permanent tribute to the heroes of 9-11. The amount of memorabilia left by the public was so large, part of it had to be stored at the University of Nevada Las Vegas's Special Collections Department.

- The Muscular Dystrophy Telethon, hosted by local resident Jerry Lewis, has been held in Las Vegas every year since 1973, except for 1990, when it was in Los Angeles for its twenty-fifth anniversary.

- The Las Vegas Hilton erected the world's largest free-standing sign in 1997 after the previous sign fell over due to high winds. It had been built with faulty steel that couldn't support the sign under the conditions. Luckily no one was injured when the sign collapsed. The new sign stands twenty stories, cost $9 million, and has more than six miles of neon and fluorescent lights.

- The Las Vegas Hilton, with 3,174 rooms and 100,000 square feet of casino space on sixty-four acres, is the largest Hilton in the world.

- Actress Carole Lombard died in 1942 when her plane crashed into Mount Potosi outside of Las Vegas. She was divorcing Clark Gable at the time.

- Actor Mickey Rooney married eight times in Las Vegas: Ava Gardner 1942, Betty Jane Rase 1944, Martha Vickers 1948, Elaine Mahnsen 1952, Barbara Thomason 1959, Marge Lane 1967, Carolyn Hockette 1969, and January Chamberlin 1978.

- The Thunderbirds, a precision military flying team that performs throughout the world, is based in Las Vegas, which is also home to the National Finals Rodeo and the World Series of Poker.

- More than 84,000 LED lights are changed in Las Vegas every year.

- In 2005 Las Vegas celebrated its one hundredth anniversary.

- When the Hoover Dam was built in the 1930s to tame the Colorado River, it created Lake Mead, the largest manmade lake in the United States. It has 550 miles of shoreline and 248 square miles of surface area. It holds 28.5 million acre feet of water and 600,000 acre feet of water is absorbed into the air each year.

- Las Vegas residents use 375 gallons of water per person. This is twice as high as Phoenix, which has higher average temperatures than Las Vegas.

- In the 1990s, Las Vegas was the fastest growing city in the nation. The valley grew by an average of four thousand people every month, increasing its population by the end of the decade by more than 85 percent. In the early 2000s, the average increased to six thousand people moving into the valley each month.

- Most of Las Vegas isn't an official town. The city of Las Vegas only extends south to Sahara Avenue, not growing much past its original plotting in 1905. The rest of Las Vegas, including almost the entire Strip, is not part of the city of Las Vegas at all. In fact, most of what is called Las Vegas is simply in Clark County and the majority of Las Vegas's residents do not live within the boundaries of the city of Las Vegas.

BIBLIOGRAPHY

SOURCES FOR LAS VEGAS FACTS AND TRIVIA

Burbank, Jeff. *Las Vegas Babylon: True Tales of Glitter, Glamour, and Greed.* Lanham, MD: M. Evans, 2008.

City of Las Vegas Web site: www.lasvegasnevada.gov/index.htm, www.lasvegasnevada.gov/FactsStatistics/funfacts.htm.

Clark County Marriage Bureau Web site: www.accessclarkcounty .com, www.accessclarkcounty.com/depts/clerk/Pages/marriage _information.aspx.

Fremont Street Experience Web site: www.vegasexperience.com.

Las Vegas Convention and Visitors Authority Web site: www.lvcva .com, www.lvcva.com/press/statistics-facts/add-sources.jsp.

Las Vegas Hilton Web site: www.lvhilton.com.

Moreno, Richard. Nevada Trivia. Baldwin Park, CA: Gem Guides Book Company, 2005.

National Park Service Web site: www.nps.gov, www.nps.gov/lame/ historyculture/index.htm.

Nevada Gaming Commission and State Gaming Control Board Web site: www.gaming.nv.gov.

New-York New-York Hotel Casino Web site: www.nynyhotel casino.com.

Stratosphere Hotel and Casino Web site: www.stratospherehotel.com.

GENERAL SOURCES

Mormons Arrive in Las Vegas—1855

Church of Jesus Christ of Latter Day Saints Web site: www.lds.org, www.lds.org/churchhistory/history.

Land, Barbara and Myrick. *A Short History of Las Vegas,* 2nd Edition. Reno: University of Nevada Press, 2004.

Mormon Historic Sites Registry Web site: www.mormonhistoric sitesregistry.org, www.mormonhistoricsitesregistry.org/USA/ nevada/lasVegas/oldMormonFort/history.htm.

National Park Service Web site: www.nps.gov, www.nps.gov/nr/ twhp/wwwlps/lessons/122fort/index.htm.

Nevada History Web site: www.nevada-history.org, www.nevada -history.org/las_vegas.html.

Nevada Division of State Parks Web site: www.parks.nv.gov, www.parks.nv.gov/olvmf.htm.

Old Las Vegas Mormon Fort State Historic Park, personal visit and observations by the author.

Public Broadcasting Service: KNPB Web site: www.knpb.org, www.knpb.org/productions/historicnevada/mormon.asp.

Vegas.com Web site: www.vegas.com/attractions, www.vegas.com/ attractions/off_the_strip/mormonfort.html.

The Sale of Las Vegas . . . Again—1905

Ainlay Jr., Thomas, Gabaldon, Judy Dixon. *Las Vegas: The Fabulous First Century.* Charleston, SC: Arcadia Publishing, 2003.

Land, Barbara and Myrick. *A Short History of Las Vegas,* 2nd Edition. Reno: University of Nevada Press, 2004.

Las Vegas Review Journal. The First 100 Web site: www.1st100 .com, www.1st100.com/part1/mcwilliams.html, www.1st100 .com/part1/wclark.html.

Moehring, Eugene P., Green, Michael S. *Las Vegas: A Centennial History.* Reno: University of Nevada Press, 2005.

This Is Sam's Town—1906

Ainlay Jr., Thomas, Gabaldon, Judy Dixon. *Las Vegas: The Fabulous First Century.* Charleston, SC: Arcadia Publishing, 2003.

Dunar, Andrew J., McBride, Dennis. *Building Hoover Dam: An Oral History of the Great Depression.* Reno: University of Nevada Press, 1993.

Land, Barbara and Myrick. *A Short History of Las Vegas,* 2nd Edition. Reno: University of Nevada Press, 2004.

Las Vegas Metropolitan Police Department Web site: www.lvmpd .com, www.lvmpd.com/about/history.html.

Las Vegas Review Journal. The First 100 Web site: www.1st100 .com, www.1st100.com/part1/gay.html.

Moehring, Eugene P., Green, Michael S. *Las Vegas: A Centennial History.* Reno: University of Nevada Press, 2005.

Special Collections, UNLV Libraries. University of Nevada Las Vegas, personal visit and observations by the author.

Bootleg Canyon—1920

Anti-Saloon League Web site: www.wpl.lib.oh.us/AntiSaloon/ index.html.

Bootleg Canyon Web site: www.bootlegcanyon.org.

Dunar, Andrew J., McBride, Dennis. *Building Hoover Dam: An Oral History of the Great Depression.* Reno: University of Nevada Press, 1993.

Ohio State University College of Humanities Web site: www .prohibition.osu.edu.

United States Constitution Online Web site: www.usconstitution .net/const.html.

University of Nevada Las Vegas College of Humanities, personal visit and observations by the author.

Wright, Frank. *Nevada Yesterdays.* Washington, D.C.: Stephens Press LLC, 2005.

Early Man Discovered in Las Vegas—1930

Harrington, M. R., "Man and Beast in Gypsum Cave," *The Desert Magazine,* April 1940.

Land, Barbara and Myrick. *A Short History of Las Vegas,* 2nd Edition. Reno: University of Nevada Press, 2004.

Las Vegas Review Journal. The First 100 Web site: www.1st100 .com, www.1st100.com/part1/harrington.html.

Minnesota State University Emuseum Web site: www.mnsu.edu/ emuseum, www.mnsu.edu/emuseum/information/biography/ fghij/harrington_mark.html.

Nevada State Museum, personal visit and observations by the author.

Online Nevada Encyclopedia Web site: www.onlinenevada.org, www.onlinenevada.org/gypsum_cave.

A Town Prepares for the Dam—1930

Ainlay Jr., Thomas, Gabaldon, Judy Dixon. *Las Vegas: The Fabulous First Century.* Charleston, SC: Arcadia Publishing, 2003.

Clark County Museum, personal visit and observations by the author.

Dunar, Andrew J., McBride, Dennis. *Building Hoover Dam: An Oral History of the Great Depression.* Reno: University of Nevada Press, 1993.

Land, Barbara and Myrick. *A Short History of Las Vegas,* 2nd Edition. Reno: University of Nevada Press, 2004.

Moehring, Eugene P., Green, Michael S. *Las Vegas: A Centennial History.* Reno: University of Nevada Press, 2005.

The First Casinos—1931

Ainlay Jr., Thomas, Gabaldon, Judy Dixon. *Las Vegas: The Fabulous First Century.* Charleston, SC: Arcadia Publishing, 2003.

History of Nevada Web site: www.clan.lib.nv.us/content.asp?id=506.

Land, Barbara and Myrick. *A Short History of Las Vegas,* 2nd Edition. Reno: University of Nevada Press, 2004.

Las Vegas Review Journal. The First 100 Web site: www.1st100 .com, www.1st100.com/part2/hull.html, www.1st100.com/ part1/stocker.html, www.1st100.com/part1/cashman.html.

Moehring, Eugene P. *Resort City in the Sunbelt 1930–2000,* 2nd Edition. Reno: University of Nevada Press, 2000.

Moehring, Eugene P., Green, Michael S. *Las Vegas: A Centennial History.* Reno: University of Nevada Press, 2005.

Online Nevada Encyclopedia Web site: www.onlinenevada.org, www.onlinenevada.org/pair_o_dice_club_and_early_las_vegas_strip.

Poker Player Newspaper Web site: www.pokerplayernewspaper. com/, www.pokerplayernewspaper.com/viewarticle.php?id=124.

Roosevelt, Eleanor. "What Ten Million Women Want," *The Home Magazine,* March 1932.

Smith, Rod. "Legalization of Betting Put Nevada on the Map and Started the Strip," *Review Journal,* March 19, 2006.

Special Collections, UNLV Libraries. University of Nevada Las Vegas, personal visit and observations by the author.

University of Nevada Las Vegas Center for Gaming Research: www.gaming.unlv.edu, www.gaming.unlv.edu/ElRanchoVegas/ story.html.

Women's Research Institute of Nevada Web site: www.wrin.unlv .edu, www.wrin.unlv.edu/biographies/stocker_mayme.html.

Vegas Helps the War Effort—1941

Condor, Albert E. *The Men Behind the Guns: The History of Enlisted Aerial Gunnery 1917–1991.* Paducah, KY: Turner Publishing Company, 1994.

Corbin, April. "Where the Fighter Pilot Calls Home," *Las Vegas Sun,* May 15, 2008.

MacGlashan Air Machine Gun Web site: www.macglashanbbgun .com, www.macglashanbbgun.com/History/Installations/tabid/ 60/Default.aspx.

McCracken, Robert D. *Las Vegas: The Great American Playground.* Reno: University of Nevada Press, 1996.

Nellis Air Force Base Web site: www.nellis.af.mil, www.strategic -air-command.com/bases/Nellis_AFB.htm.

Online Nevada Encyclopedia Web site: www.onlinenevada.org, www.onlinenevada.org/Las_Vegas_Army_Air_Base.

Public Broadcasting Web site: www.pbs.org, www.pbs.org/wgbh/amex/lasvegas/peopleevents/e_federalprojects.html.

Block 16 Comes to an End—1941

Dunar, Andrew J., McBride, Dennis. *Building Hoover Dam: An Oral History of the Great Depression.* Reno: University of Nevada Press, 1993.

Nellis Air Force Base Web site: www.nellis.af.mil.

Nevada State Museum, personal visit and observations by the author.

Online Nevada Encyclopedia Web site: www.onlinenevada.org, www.onlinenevada.org/las_vegas__block_16.

Special Collections, UNLV Libraries, University of Nevada Las Vegas, personal visit and observations by the author.

The Mob Comes to Town—1945

Ainlay Jr., Thomas, Gabaldon, Judy Dixon. *Las Vegas: The Fabulous First Century.* Charleston, SC: Arcadia Publishing, 2003.

Bugsy Siegel Web site: www.bugsysiegel.net.

Dearly Departed: The Tragical History Tour Web site: www.dearlydepartedtours.com, www.dearlydepartedtours.com/Deceased/s/bugsy/bugsysiegel.htm.

Federal Bureau of Investigation of Bugsy Siegel: www.foia.fbi.gov/siegel/siegel1c.pdf.

Land, Barbara and Myrick. *A Short History of Las Vegas,* 2nd Edition. Reno: University of Nevada Press, 2004.

Las Vegas Now Web site: George Knapp interview with Joe Yablonsky and Oscar Goodman, www.klas-tv.com/Global/story.asp?S=649655.

Las Vegas Review Journal. The First 100 Web site: www.1st100.com, www.1st100.com/part2/siegel.html.

Moehring, Eugene P. *Resort City in the Sunbelt 1930–2000,* 2nd Edition. Reno: University of Nevada Press, 2000.

Public Broadcasting Web site: www.pbs.org, www.pbs.org/wgbh/amex/lasvegas/peopleevents/p_siegel.html.

Turkus, Burton B., Feder, Sid. *Murder, Inc.: The Story of the Syndicate.* Cambridge, MA: Da Capo Press, 2003.

A Mushroom-Shaped Cloud in the Distance—1951

Ainlay Jr., Thomas, Gabaldon, Judy Dixon. *Las Vegas: The Fabulous First Century.* Charleston, SC: Arcadia Publishing, 2003.

The Atomic Testing Museum, personal visit and observations by the author.

Basten, Fred E., Phoenix, Charles. *Fabulous Las Vegas in the 50s: Glitz, Glamour & Games.* Santa Monica, CA: Angel City Press, 1999.

Clark County Museum, personal visit and observations by the author.

Land, Barbara and Myrick. *A Short History of Las Vegas,* 2nd Edition. Reno: University of Nevada Press, 2004.

Public Broadcasting Web site: www.pbs.org, www.pbs.org/wgbh/amex/lasvegas/peopleevents/e_atomictourism.html.

U.S. Department of Energy National Nuclear Security Administration Web site: www.nv.doe.gov, www.nv.doe.gov/library/factsheets/DOENV_1024.pdf.

A Five-Month Showdown—1951

The Good Gambling Guide Web site: www.thegoodgambling guide.co.uk, www.thegoodgamblingguide.co.uk/spotlight/ players/nickthegreek.htm.

Launch Poker Web site: www.launchpoker.com, www.launchpoker .com/players/poker_players/-nicholas-nick-the-greek-dandolos-/, www.launchpoker.com/players/wsop_winners/1970_1980/ -johnny-moss-/.

Las Vegas Review Journal. The First 100 Web site: www.1st100 .com, www.1st100.com/part2/binion.html.

Poker Listings Web site: www.pokerlistings.com, www.poker listings.com/poker-player_johnny-moss?show=bio#pp-bio.

Poker Player Newspaper Web site: www.pokerplayernewspaper .com/, www.pokerplayernewspaper.com/viewarticle.php?id=124, www.pokerplayernewspaper.com/viewarticle.php?id=1400/.

Professional Poker Web site: www.professional-poker.com, www.professional-poker.com/poker-players/johnny-moss.htm.

Unknown Poker Web site: www.unknownpoker.com, www.unknownpoker.com/players/nick-dandelos.htm.

The King Bombs—1956

Elvis: The Official Site of the King of Rock and Roll Web site: www.elvis.com.

Elvis Presley News Web site: www.elvispresleynews.com, www.elvispresleynews.com/ElvisWeddingPhotos.html.

Land, Barbara and Myrick. *A Short History of Las Vegas,* 2nd Edition. Reno: University of Nevada Press, 2004.

Las Vegas Hilton: www.lvhilton.com.

Scotty Moore Web site: www.scottymoore.net, www.scottymoore
.net/vegas56.html.

A Search for Showgirls—1957

Las Vegas Review Journal. The First 100 Web site: www.1st100
.com, www.1st100.com/part2/sinatra.html.

Special Collections, UNLV Libraries, University of Nevada Las
Vegas: Sands Hotel Collection, Virginia James Interview,
Denise Clair Garon Interview, Carmon Messwab Interview.

The Summit—1960

Land, Barbara and Myrick. *A Short History of Las Vegas,* 2nd
Edition. Reno: University of Nevada Press, 2004.

Schoell, William, Quirk, Lawrence J. *The Rat Pack: Neon
Lights with the Kings of Cool.* New York: Taylor Publishing
Company, 1998.

Special Collections, UNLV Libraries, University of Nevada Las
Vegas: www.library.nevada.edu/speccol/dino/ratpack.html.

A Mysterious Billionaire Refuses to Leave—1966

Ainlay Jr., Thomas, Gabaldon, Judy Dixon. *Las Vegas: The Fabulous
First Century.* Charleston, SC: Arcadia Publishing, 2003.

Land, Barbara and Myrick. *A Short History of Las Vegas,* 2nd
Edition. Reno: University of Nevada Press, 2004.

Las Vegas Review Journal. The First 100 Web site: www.1st100
.com, www.1st100.com/part3/hughes.html.

Moehring, Eugene P. *Resort City in the Sunbelt 1930–2000,*
2nd Edition. Reno: University of Nevada Press, 2000.

Public Broadcasting Web site: www.pbs.org, www.pbs.org/wgbh/
amex/lasvegas/peopleevents/p_hughes.html.

Special Collections, UNLV Libraries, University of Nevada Las Vegas: www.digital.library.unlv.edu/hughes/index.html.

An Evel Jump—1967

Caesars Palace Web site: www.caesarspalace.com.

Evel Knievel Web site: www.evelknievel.com, www.evelknievel.com/american-icon.html.

Land, Barbara and Myrick. *A Short History of Las Vegas,* 2nd Edition. Reno: University of Nevada Press, 2004.

Malnic, Eric. "He Lived Life on a Dare," *Los Angeles Times,* December 1, 2007.

Ross, Christopher. *Evel Knievel and Wide World of Sports: A Winning Combination.* ABC Sports: www.espn.go.com/abc sports/wwos/e_knievel.html.

A Casino Catches Fire—1980

Arnett, Peter. "How it Happened: Fire Got Lots of Help From People," *Review Journal,* November 23, 1980.

Broderick, Chris. Untitled, *Review Journal,* November 23, 1980.

Clark County Fire Department: MGM Fire Investigation.

Review Journal, "Makeshift Morgue Pressed into Service," November 22, 1980.

Scripps, Cynthia. "MGM Hotel Rescuer Unidentified," *Review Journal,* November 22, 1980.

The Casino Industry Gets a Makeover—1988

Eisner, Michael. Interview with Steve Wynn on CNBC: www.veoh.com/videos/v375817wEdcmpT2.

Land, Barbara and Myrick. *A Short History of Las Vegas,* 2nd Edition. Reno: University of Nevada Press, 2004.

Las Vegas Review Journal. The First 100 Web site: www.1st100
.com, www.1st100.com/part3/wynn.html.

Mirage Las Vegas Web site: www.mirage.com.

Moehring, Eugene P., Green, Michael S. *Las Vegas: A Centennial
History.* Reno: University of Nevada Press, 2005.

PEPCON Explosion—1988

Bates, Warren. "Shattered Windows, Lives," *Review Journal,* May
3, 1998.

The History Channel: *Inviting Disaster.* DVD set.

Review Journal Web site: www.reviewjournal.com, www.review
journal.com/news/pepcon/.

Rogers, Keith. "Remnants of Explosion Linger," *Review Journal,*
May 3, 1998.

Hell on the Streets—1992

Johnson, Dirk. "After the Riots; Mob Violence Continues in Las
Vegas," *The New York Times,* May 19, 1992.

Las Vegas Sun, "King Riot's Impact Still Questioned," April 26, 2002.

Linder, Doug. "The Trials of Los Angeles Police Officers in
Connection with the Beating of Rodney King," University of
Missouri–Kansas City School of Law, 2001.

Scott, Cathy. "Rioting Led to Changes in West Las Vegas,"
Las Vegas Sun, April 30, 1977.

Gang Members Terrorize the Strip—1994

Dahlberg, Tim. "LA Gangs Tab Casinos as Cash Targets,"
The Press-Enterprise, March 10, 1994.

Geer, Carri. "Gang Members Sentenced for Roles in Casino
Robbery," *Review Journal,* April 19, 1997.

Huang, Carole. "Aladdin Heist Van Located," *Review Journal*, February 24, 1994.

Katz, Jesse. "L.A. Gangs Find Vegas an Easy Hit—So Far," *The Seattle Times*, May 30, 1994.

Palermo, Dave. "New Heist May Bring Back Bars," *Review Journal*, April 23, 1994.

Palermo, Dave. "Las Vegas Police Link Casino Holdups Law Officers, Security Chiefs To Discuss Recent Cage Heists," *Review Journal*, April 26, 1994.

Pringle, Paul. "All Bets Off," *The Tampa Tribune*, July 3, 1994.

Smith, John. "A Few Bandit Barriers in the Casinos Wouldn't Hurt Anyone," *Review Journal*, April 28, 1994.

Robertson, Alonza. "Police Catch Five Suspects in Armed Robbery of Harrah's," *Review Journal*, April 25, 1994.

The One Hundred Year Flood—1999

Koch, Ed, Radke, Jace. "Damage Assessed, Area Braces for More Rain," *Las Vegas Sun*, July 9, 1999.

National Weather Service: *The Las Vegas Flash Floods of 8 July 1999: A Post-Event Summary*. Published November 9, 1999.

USA Today, "Las Vegas Swamped by Killer Flood," July 9, 1999.

U.S. Department of the Interior U.S. Geological Survey: Flood of July 8, 1999, in Las Vegas Valley, Southern Nevada, July 2000.

Tiger Attack on the Strip—2003

Adams, Cindy. "Siegfried & Roy on a Long Journey," *New York Post*, May 28, 2008.

Kalil, J. M., Berns, Dave. "Tiger Attacks Roy Onstage," *Review Journal*, October 4, 2003.

KVBC News 3 TV Web site: www.kvbc.com,
www.kvbc.com/Global/category.asp?C=45924.

Marquez, Miguel. "Roy of Siegfried and Roy Critical After
Mauling," CNN, October 4, 2003.

Siegfried and Roy Official Web site: www.siegfriedandroy.com,
www.siegfriedandroy.com/biography/index.php.

A British Battleship Blows Up the Dunes—2003

Sebelius, Steve. "Tower Tumbles into Dust," *Las Vegas Sun,*
October 28, 1993.

Vegas Today and Tomorrow: Las Vegas Implosions: Video:
www.vegastodayandtomorrow.com/implode.htm.

INDEX

ABOUT THE AUTHOR

Paul Papa is a full-time writer who has worked as a security officer at several Las Vegas casinos. While working as a hotel investigator, he began writing true stories about uncommon events. He now concentrates on non-fiction, technical, and commercial writing and lives in Las Vegas.